2·95

Perspectives on Residential Child Care

An Annotated Bibliography

Research and other literature in the United States, Canada and Great Britain 1966-74

Hilary Prosser

NFER Publishing Company Ltd.

D1795898

B 2 251247 0

Published by the NFER Publishing Company Ltd.,
2 Jennings Buildings, Thames Avenue,
Windsor, Berks. SL4 1QS.
Registered Office: The Mere, Upton Park, Slough, Berks. SL1 2DQ.
First published in 1976
© National Children's Bureau, 1976
ISBN 0 85633 113 9

Typeset by Cameographics Ltd.,
63 Milford Road, Reading, Berks.

John Gardner (Printers), Hawthorne Road, Bootle, Merseyside L20 6JX
Distributed in the USA by Humanities Press Inc.,
Atlantic Highlands, New Jersey 07716 USA.

Contents

INTRODUCTION

It is now nine years since the publication of *Residential Child Care —
Facts and Fallacies* (Dinnage, R. and Pringle, M.K., 1967, Longman).
The current review brings the volume of research work up to date as far
as the end of 1974 and also includes some impressionistic material
gathered from books and from numerous articles in journals devoted to
child care. In either case only literature published after 1966 has been
reviewed. The field covered is specifically that of residential child care
but it excludes the care of handicapped children — either the physically
or the mentally handicapped — in special homes or in special residential
schools. Handicapped children are referred to in this review only when
they are compared, in the literature, with normal children; specific work
concerning the care and treatment of handicapped children in care has
not been reviewed. The care of children in community schools has also
been excluded. While the importance of these two groups is not dis-
counted, time limits unfortunately made it impossible to encompass
the great deal of work that has been done in these areas in recent years.

The information presented here provides detailed summaries of the
relevant research literature — specifying the scope and purpose of the
study, its sample, methodology and findings — and somewhat shorter
accounts of the impressionistic material. The research literature is
divided into four sections dealing with the consequences of residential
care for children; the characteristics of children in care; evaluations of
their care and treatment; and aspects of residential staff, their training
and conditions of service. In each section the reviews appear in alpha-
betical order by author.

The impressionistic material has been grouped under three headings
dealing with Policy and Practice; Residential Child Care Staff and
Historical Considerations.

I should like to acknowledge the assistance of Ian Vallender —
Librarian at the National Children's Bureau — who traced and obtained
much of the material, and of Peter Wedge who helped with the planning
stage, devoted a great deal of time to reading through the manuscript
and made many constructive comments which were much appreciated.

This project was funded by a grant from the Noel Buxton Trust,
without whose generous support it would not have been possible.

Overview

Who are the Children in Care?

Firstly, how many children are 'in care'? The most recent available statistics show that in 1973 there were 115,600 children in care of local authorities in the United Kingdom. This represents a considerable increase, the scale of which can be measured by comparing the figures in England and Wales for 1961, 1966 and 1970, which were approximaterialy 62,000, 69,000 and 71,000 respectively. Legislative changes in the classification of Approved Schools, etc., led to a further increase in 1971 (to 87,400) which by 1974 had reached 95,900.

Of all the children in care the proportion with foster parents, as distinct from those in local authority children's homes, voluntary homes, etc. varied as between England and Wales, Scotland and Northern Ireland. Of all children in care in England in 1973, just over one-third were living in residential accommodation — i.e. local authority children's homes, voluntary homes, hostels and accommodation for the handicapped, but not remand homes and approved schools (*Health and Personal Social Services Statistics for England*, HMSO, 1974). Although the figures for other parts of the United Kingdom vary, it is clear that large proportions of children who are in care spend considerable time in residential accommodation throughout the United Kingdom.

Of all children admitted to the care of local authorities in 1973 official statistics show that almost one-third were received as a result of parental short-term illness and mother's confinement in hospital and that they generally stayed only a few weeks. Abandonment, mother's death or desertion accounted for a further ten per cent of admissions; illegitimacy — three per cent; homelessness and unsatisfactory home conditions — eleven per cent and children subject to care orders — thirty per cent. Various other reasons accounted for the admission of the remaining thirteen per cent of children.

Of the children who may only come into care for a relatively short-term, usually as a consequence of some short-term crisis situation in the family, little has been documented. Official statistics for England and Wales do show however a substantial drop in the proportion of children admitted to care on a short-term basis. Whereas in 1967 approximately half of all admissions to care were regarded as short-term placements owing to mother's confinement or illness of parent or guardian, in 1973 this proportion had fallen to approximately thirty per cent of all admissions (*Health and Personal Social Services Statistics*, HMSO, 1974). Homelessness, mother's illlness or mother's confinement in hospital are among the most common reasons for short-term admission to care. These are not necessarily once and for all occurrences and it may well be that many children come in and out of care on several occasions. The available evidence suggests, however, that application for care because of the mother's admission to hospital is rarely the result of just temporary practical difficulties encountered by a family otherwise functioning satisfactorily and that often it signifies a more fundamental inability of the family to cope, expressed in such diverse ways as poor community integration, rigid conjugal role segregation and lack of supportive contact with the extended family (Schaffer and Schaffer, 1968; Mapstone, 1969).

Those children, who for some period of their lives receive some form of long-term substitute residential care, have been broadly divided by Rowe and Lambert (1973) into two distinct categories — (a) single, illegitimate children who tend to come into care as babies, have little contact with their parents and stay a very long time unless adopted, and (b) sibling groups from disorganized families, who tend to come in and out of care more often, have more contact with their parents and are less likely to remain in care throughout their childhood (Rowe and Lambert, 1973). Other recent studies which examined the characteristics of children in long-term care suggest that the principle reasons for their admission include abandonment; mother's death or desertion; parental long-term illness, particularly mental illness; and commital under a Fit Persons Order (Walton and Heywood, 1971; Shapiro, 1968 a and b). As regards the children in long-term care, the evidence of the above studies suggests that substantial proportions are illegitimate, or are coloured or half caste, have a mental or physical handicap or a behaviour problem, or have less than average educational attainment.

Of course, not all children in long-term residential care need, or are thought suitable for, a substitute family, either in an adoptive home or in a foster home. Rowe and Lambert (1973), for instance, found that only twenty-two per cent of their study children were thought by their social workers to need a substitute family, although the proportion in different child care agencies varied from three per cent to forty-five per cent. Children in need of substitute families were characterized in this study by sex, age, colour, behaviour problems, physical handicaps and below average intelligence. Furthermore, of the obstacles to placement, as seen by social workers, the most frequently mentioned was the problem of finding homes for groups of brothers and sisters.

Studies which have been carried out with special groups of children in care provide some evidence concerning the circumstances of coloured children in long-term care and of illegitimate children in care (Pinder and Shaw, 1974; Shapiro, 1968 a and b).

An exploratory study to investigate the circumstances of coloured children in long-term care found that, at the time of their admission, only a minority came from what would be regarded as normal, intact families with married parents living together (Pinder and Shaw, 1974). Fewer than one child in five had been living with both parents. The majority of coloured children were born in the UK, and the great majority of immigrant parents had been living in the UK for at least two years prior to the child's admission to care. These findings, it is suggested, seem to explode certain myths which have common currency in social work circles: that coloured children are immigrant children; that they come into care quickly after arrival in this country because of 'culture shock'; and that coloured families break down because the parent/child bond has been weakened by separation, the result of parents arriving years in advance of their children and sending for them later.

The same study also throws some light on the attitudes of field-workers and caring agents (residential staff and foster parents) towards coloured children 'in care'. Fieldworkers appeared to know very little about the children on their caseloads and, in general, they saw coloured children's families as particularly unhelpful to the child. Both residential staff and foster parents, perhaps because they knew them better, tended to view coloured children more favourably than fieldworkers and to see them as less 'problematic' than non-coloured children; they made less distinction than did fieldworkers between coloured and non-coloured families in terms of their value to the children.

A small study of illegitimate children in long-term care showed that eighty-six per cent of them were under the age of five years when first admitted to care, one-half were under the age of one year and one-fifth were less than one month old. The two most important factors in reasons for their admission were abandonment by the mother and the mother's mental incapacity — over one-half of the children were accounted for under these two categories (Shapiro, 1968 a).

A further study of illegitimate coloured children in long-term care shows that one-half had been deserted by their mothers, compared with only one-quarter of white children in the sample; that rather more coloured children than white children were aged under five years on admission to care; and that the proportion of coloured putative fathers who were showing some interest in their children was greater than that of white putative fathers.

These findings, from somewhat limited investigations, point up a number of questions. Is enough being done, for example, to help newly arrived immigrants? Are there adequate family planning services and, more importantly, are they reaching those people most in need? What kind of services are available to unmarried mothers, both those who wish to keep their babies and others who seek adoption for them? In short, are there sufficient support services to reduce the need for residential care among this group?

The American literature in this field is sparse and, in the main, is confined to the emotional and psychiatric health of children admitted to residential care. Pappenfort and Kilpatrick (1969), for example, in a national survey of over two thousand public and private children's residential institutions in the United States, show that three-quarters of all children in institutions were believed to be emotionally disturbed. Of these children thirteen per cent of those in institutions specifically for the emotionally disturbed were being seen regularly by psychiatrists, and in other types of institutions the proportion ranged from one per cent of children in detention to three per cent of those in homes for the dependent and neglected.

Evidence concerning the prevalence of disturbed adolescent children in care suggests that the populations of treatment centres in the United States are changing significantly in the direction of more severe disturbance (Weintrob, 1974). It was found that psychiatric hospitals had become the major referral source and that the major diagnostic category had shifted from personality disorders to schizophrenia.

The Consequences of Residential Care for Children

Since the early studies of Bowlby, Spitz, Goldfarb and others which first presented the effects of maternal deprivation, a great deal of research concerned with the consequences of residential care for children has been generated both in the United States and in Western Europe. 'Maternal deprivation' has been held to cause conditions as diverse as mental subnormality, delinquency, depression, dwarfism, acute distress and affectionless psychopathy (Bowlby, 1951; Ainsworth, 1962). However, it now seems evident that the experiences included under the term 'maternal deprivation' are too heterogeneous and the effects too varied for it to continue to have any real usefulness (Rutter, 1972). Given the limited scale of most studies and the resulting lack of sound data about the effects of institutional care upon children, Rutter believes it is inappropriate to draw any firm conclusions from them although there does seem general agreement that 'bad' care of children in early life can have 'bad' effects both short-term and long-term. When summarizing research evidence, it was concluded by Dinnage and Pringle in 1967 that 'prolonged institutionalization during the early years of life leaves a child very vulnerable to later stress' and today there appears to be no new evidence which contradicts this.

1. Studies of infants and young children

Surprisingly few studies have been carried out in recent years into the effects of institutionalization upon infants and young children. The data available in Britain seem to suggest that, as far as cognitive development is concerned, what matters is not whether the child is in an institution or not, but rather the type of care he or she receives. Whereas many earlier studies have documented the impaired language, poor intelligence and disturbed behaviour which frequently occur in children who have been reared in institutions, these are not found in all children coming from all institutions. Recent findings are contradictory. Children reared in the best residential nurseries, where there is a good level of cognitive stimulation and child care, do not show any significant intellectual retardation although their social development may be restricted. The Tizards, for example, found that residential nursery children were significantly less friendly than children reared in their own homes and that while they had fewer social experiences and less contact with adults there was no significant intellectual or language retardation at three years (Tizard and Tizard, 1971), although perhaps some slight retardation at two years (Tizard and Joseph, 1970). The major area of difference in the development of residential nursery children compared with that of a group of working class children brought up in their own homes lay in their relationships with their caretakers and with strangers. Nursery children were less willing to approach or to stay alone with strangers, and, with familiar adults they were, in certain situations, more clinging. A variety of possible explanations for the typical behaviour of nursery children has been advanced — they include the lack of neighbourhood experiences of nursery children compared with children living in their own homes, the multiplicity of their caretakers and peer contacts and the more limited emotional involvement of caretakers. It is suggested that the children's relationships with one another and with adults change as they get older, and that the nature of this social relationship depends on the specific manner in which residential care is organized rather than on 'institutional care' as such. As was argued by Dinnage and Pringle in their literature review (1967), considerable improvements can be brought about by drastically reducing the number of people concerned with the daily care and handling of infants, by ensuring continuity of 'caretaker' and by introducing a carefully planned 'enriched' and 'therapeutic' environment from the earliest years onwards. However, little improvement seems to have been effected. It has also been shown that having a 'reliable, consistent friend outside' is associated with better emotional and social adjustment (*Deprivation and Education*, Pringle, 1965) but little is still known about factors within institutional life associated with a better or worse social adjustment and the key question of which institutional features lead to language deficit, intellectual retardation and behavioural disturbance remains a matter for further research.

That no firm conclusions can be drawn about the effects of institutional care on young children is emphasized by the findings of an Israeli study which stand in stark contrast to those of the Tizards (Kohen-Raz, 1968). In this study a group of infants who had been reared in a kibbutz were compared for mental and other development with a group of institutionalized children and a group of children living in their own homes. The children raised in kibbutzim residential nurseries, but who retained strong links with their parents, showed no adverse effects, but the children raised in institutions were conspicuously retarded in both areas when compared with the other groups.

An Australian study of the effects of own home- and institution-rearing on the behavioural development of young normal and mongol children found that institution-reared normal children were behaviourally more retarded than their home-reared counterparts of the same chronological age. Although they had good supplies of toys the institution-reared children showed less object-oriented behaviour and less visual attention to objects than did home reared children when compared on the basis of developmental level, and they were more retarded in their sensorimotor development (Francis, 1971).

2. Studies of older children

'The two potentially most damaging aspects of residential care are that a psychologically, culturally and educationally restricted, impoverished or, at worst, even depriving substitute environment may unintentionally be provided; secondly that unless special steps are taken, children may grow up without a personal sense of identity, lacking a coherent picture of both their past and their future,' (Dinnage and Pringle, 1967).

In general, recent research relating to the ill-effects of institutional care on older children has been concerned with social and emotional development rather than with intellectual or educational development. It is clear from these studies that children in care are more likely to exhibit behavioural disturbance or mixed antisocial/neurotic disorder than children living in their own homes, although the picture is complicated by other factors such as family background, sex, age when first admitted to care and length of stay in care.

Wolkind and Rutter (1973), for example, suggest that children experiencing short-term institutional care are 'at risk' of antisocial disorder, not so much because of the effect of the care *per se,* but rather because such children are liable to come from disturbed families. Studies into the development of antisocial behaviour in children show the importance of family relationships and, on the whole, the evidence suggests that children who have had the most favourable home environments are least affected by deprivation and that those who have least to lose are most affected (Rutter, 1972).

A psychiatric study of a group of children in a long-stay institution, examined the relationships between some features of 'affectionless psychopathy' and factors in the child's family and experience; it was found that antisocial behaviour was related to aspects in the child's family but that superficial overfriendliness was related to an early admission to care (Wolkind, 1974 a).

Surprisingly, little attention has been paid to differences between boys' and girls' responses to residential care, although a recent study in this area found important sex differences in the development of antisocial disorder among children in institutions (Wolkind, 1974). Family factors, such as lack of contact with a father and large family size were found to relate significantly to antisocial disorder in boys, but not in girls. Conversely, early admission to care does not appear to be an aetiological factor in antisocial disorder in boys, but for girls there was found a positive relationship between prolonged early experience of residential care and antisocial disorder.

It is concluded from these findings that to attempt at all costs to keep a child with its own family may not be the way to prevent the development of psychiatric disorders, since many children appear to be severely damaged by their experiences prior to admission. Attempts must be made instead to identify the factors within the residential home which are likely to cause further damage to the child after its admission, as well as factors likely to lead to some measure of recovery.

A further study demonstrates that children in care are more likely to be maladjusted than their peers living in their own homes but also shows that there is little to support the argument that the age at which a child first leaves home or the number of surrogate homes he has had as a result of separation from his own family, are related to later behaviour. Only slight evidence was found to support the view that the greater the length of current stay the child experiences, the more likely the child will be rated as maladjusted (Yule and Raynes, 1972).

Despite the evidence relating to antisocial disorder and behavioural disturbance there is little to suggest that children in residential care are any less emotionally sensitive than children in normal homes (Cheyne and Jahoda, 1971). A study designed to test this, using children's responses to voice recordings, found no clear-cut deficiency in emotional sensitivity between the two groups and it is concluded from this somewhat negative finding that the development of emotional sensitivity is related more to general perceptual and intellectual factors than to specific emotional experiences.

On the other hand, there is some evidence to suggest that children in long-term care are retarded not only in their emotional development but also in terms of social development, particularly in adolescence (Rosen, 1971a). Compared with children living in their own homes, teenagers in residential children's homes are seen by staff to be very much retarded in personal independence; they tend to be overprotected, have less freedom of movement, be more closely supervised and less adept in money matters (Rosen, 1971b). If this is so, then it would seem that one of the major aims of contemporary residential child care — to provide the child with an environment as like to that of a normal home as possible — is confounded by the effects of overprotection which set the child in care apart from other children. It would also imply that the adolescent in care is being ill-prepared for an independent life in the outside world.

Further evidence concerning the effects of institutional care on adolescents comes from an American study designed to determine whether girls in residential care differed in the process of establishing an appropriate sexual identity from girls who had continued to live in their parental homes with their biological mothers (Steele, 1971). Using measures of conscious and unconscious femininity it was found that the institution girls as a group scored consistently lower than did the girls living in their own homes, and that problems in sexual identification and ego identity tended to be extended into later adolescence among the institution group while girls living with their biological mothers expressed fewer and less severe problems in these areas and tended to exhibit such difficulties at an earlier age.

What Kind of Care Works?

In the earlier review (Dinnage and Pringle, 1967) stress was laid upon the need for research into residential child care to change its direction. It was reported that the main focus in past years had been on the effects of deprivation and institutionalization on the child's development and that having shown these to be generally detrimental, research should now concentrate on how best to ameliorate unfavourable consequences. It is regrettable that this statement is as relevant today as it was nearly ten years ago.

In Britain very little study has been made of the effects of different types of care upon different types of children; research has not been concerned with evaluating methods of care and comparative studies of institutions and other types of care have been largely ignored. There has, for example, been no evaluative comparison of the development of young children in areas where foster homes are provided for almost all, with that of children in areas where residential nurseries have been retained. It is well known that many small scale schemes are being pioneered in different local areas but, for the most part, they are undocumented. British research into residential care has been more concerned with tests of emotional and social adjustment and of intellectual achievement than with trying to discover what kind of care works and for whom. In North America evaluation of this kind is far more common although in general the emphasis is on the care and treatment of emotionally disturbed children.

One Canadian study of young children in care considered whether the development of children reared in an institution is so distorted as to cause permanent damage, and assessed the degree to which deprivation can be relieved (Flint, 1967). Over a four year period a group of infants and young children living in a residential home were studied before, during and after a period of treatment. In the light of some initial findings and recommendations the children's home was reorganized and sweeping environmental changes were made. The staff/child ratio was improved, a large group of volunteer 'mothers' were recruited and trained, and a new programme of treatment was devised.

The children's reactions to the new programme were recorded on 'Infant and Pre-School Security Scales' — previously developed at the Institute of Child Study, Toronto University — and after the first year of treatment a marked improvement was reported in many of the children. The treatment programme demonstrated the degree to which children with greatly differing personalities can respond to an enriched environment and it is concluded that four important principles must be maintained if an institution is to promote healthy development; these are — individuality of treatment, fostering of dependent relationships, provision of opportunities for initiative in the children and consistency of care and discipline.

Much of the American literature in the residential field is concerned with the care and treatment of emotionally disturbed children and with the evaluation of specific issues. These include, for example, the use of psychodramatic techniques in dealing with the everyday living problems of children in a residential centre (Geiser, 1971); the implementation of a treatment programme based on the 'operant conditioning model' for children with emotional and/or behavioural problems (Pizzat, 1973); and the effects of a short-term therapeutic programme for children with behaviour problems (Rawson, 1973).

Although a great deal of research has been documented in the United States concerning the care and treatment of these emotionally disturbed children, the studies have been mostly limited to the experience of one particular residential centre and to one particular aspect of treatment. As in Britain, comparative studies of different types of care have been ignored, and in the absence of larger studies based on national rather than local samples, generalizations cannot therefore be made.

Isolated studies here have investigated, for example, the use of 'time-out rooms', frequently referred to as control rooms, seclusion and quiet rooms, as a treatment technique in residential centres (Endres and Goke, 1973); the differences found in the kind of care provided in residential cottages on the same campus (Polsky and Claster, 1968); the attempts made by one particular residential treatment centre for emotionally disturbed children to integrate the therapeutic approach with the positive aspects of community life (Mora, Talmadge, Bryant and Hayden, 1969); and the residential treatment response of disturbed children using serial ratings of adjustment assessed by child care staff (Alderton, 1972).

One particularly interesting study, although again only local, shows the way in which transitional homes can be used in the treatment centre to group homes containing four or five children and one or two foster parents. The group home experience is described as a transitional one, bridging the gap between the time of a child's readiness to leave the treatment centre and the time of his readiness to return to his family, or live independently. As such, it is thought to provide a protective environment in which the child can gain support and strength and can renew his acquaintance with parents on a more realistic basis than the institutional climate would permit.

Casework with parents is also described in the American literature. One study, for example, describes the work of a treatment centre for emotionally disturbed boys which has been experimenting with ways in which to involve parents in the treatment of children in its care (Heiting, 1971). Parents were invited to participate in a pre-placement conference, and throughout the child's stay were encouraged to participate in the treatment programme. Although the results of this parent involvement programme cannot be accurately assessed, over a four year period there was a gradual decrease in the average length of stay at the centre.

A further study describes a 12-week parent group counselling programme carried out in Virginia, USA (Criss and Goodwin, 1970). Weekly sessions were held with parents in an effort to give them a chance to examine their relationships with their children and with themselves. It was considered by the therapists involved that after six months counselling there were signs of parents making significant efforts towards change in several of the families. It is implied from this that the child care service has a responsibility to move further into the treatment of parents while their children are in residential care, group homes or foster care.

In Britain, only one recent study has concerned itself with a comparison of different types of residential experience (Keyte, 1974). This small survey, designed to examine aspects of the residential care situation revealed by interviews with children from four different establishments and with some of their parents, found that there were marked differences in the response to questions from children placed in different establishments and that these differences were largely accounted for by differences in staff attitudes. Findings concerning the children's parents showed that their knowledge of their children's way of life, daily routine, interests and contacts, varied considerably. In general, parents appeared to be bewildered about the lack of real contact with residential social workers — more than one half had not been told about the establishment before the child was placed there and although residential staff were thought to be readily available to parents, only a very small minority were satisfied with the information given about their children.

Residential Staff

Fundamental to the quality of residential care provided at any one time is the quality of staff employed. In Britain the shortage of residential child care staff, the high rate of staff turnover and the difficulties of recruiting the right people for residential work are well recognized, were widely reported by Dinnage and Pringle in the previous review (1967) and have been repeatedly referred to in the literature for many years.

Much of this literature is impressionistic rather than statistical but there does seem to be some general agreement that among the reasons for the present shortage of staff are the long hours of work (often more thn 60 hours per week), inadequate salary scales, the demands made by the nature of the work, poor and cramped living accommodation, lack of privacy and the loneliness and isolation that can be experienced by both houseparents and their assistants (Scottish Children's Officers Association, 1967; Dr Barnardo's, 1968; Central Council for Education and Training in Social Work, 1974). The majority of residential staff are still untrained, a factor which in itself contributes towards the unattractiveness and low status of the work (Central Council for Education and Training in Social Work, 1974). A further disadvantage is seen to be the lack of adequate involvement by residential workers in developing and implementing the care and treatment plan of the child, and the lack of opportunities within a definite career structure. It is thought that, because of this situation, some residential staff believe that the only way of promotion lies in their becoming field social workers (Dr Barnardo's, 1968).

Clearly, in a number of respects, there have been large differences in both status and salary between residential and field staff and undoubtedly these discrepancies have contributed to the frequently expressed conflict between social workers and residential workers in children's homes. Although social workers and residential staff have a common aim of helping the child, they effect that aim in different ways, and their different tasks can clash. Social workers, for example, are sometimes considered to disrupt the orderly routine of the home and to present themselves as threatening figures to the houseparent, whose lack of professional status or career structure only serves to exacerbate the situation.

In terms of their respective responsibilities there now seems to be little justification for the inferiority — in status and salary — ascribed to residential as against field workers (Jillings, 1967; Barter, 1970). What is needed, it is argued, is some method of realistic cooperation which takes into account the different tasks of each side. A more satisfactory relationship between the two groups of workers can perhaps only be achieved by developing a code of common values and shared training programmes as well as by raising the general conditions of work and the salaries of residential staff.

This point is pressed by the working party of the Central Council for Education and Training in Social Work, which was set up to report on education for residential social work (1974). It is also recommended that the same salary scales should apply for all social workers but that residential workers should be appointed at points substantially higher on the scales, because of the added responsibilities and inconveniences of their work. The majority of the working party favoured a two-tier pattern of training, the first tier of which would lead to a certificate which would be a recognized national qualification but would be inferior to the second-tier qualification which would be the Certificate of Qualification in Social Work.

Elsewhere it is suggested that, in view of the large numbers of workers urgently needed in the residential field, it is unrealistic to expect that all of them could undertake a full professional training and therefore different levels of training must be provided (Winnicott, 1971). It is argued that a complete professional training programme could, for example, consist of four parts:

1. Pre-qualifying in-service study and training.
2. Qualifying training at a college or university.
3. Post-qualifying training by means of internal and external staff development programmes.
4. Advanced course of study at a university, leading to a higher qualification or a degree.

Clearly, more research is needed not only to evaluate different kinds of training programmes but also to discover the characteristics which differentiate homes with the lowest and highest rate of staff turnover. The need for more evidence in this area was stressed in the previous literature review (Dinnage and Pringle, 1967) but once again the intervening period has seen little substantial progress and the questions remain unanswered.

Apart from considerations of service and training for residential staff, some reseach has also been concerned with the personalities and attitudes of residential social workers compared with those of field workers. A study designed to evaluate how much the division between field and residential social workers can be attributed to 'differences in personality' found that, taking into account the effects of age and sex, residential workers were significantly more 'conservative' than field workers (Tutt, 1972). A further survey of students on a residential child care course and students on a field social work course found that while both groups were no more extrovert or introvert than the normal population, field social work students were found to be a fairly normally stable group emotionally but residential work students revealed a very strong and consistent shift from the normal, in an unstable direction. They also showed evidence of great feelings of anxiety, inferiority and guilt, coupled with a strong need for support, approval and acceptance (More, 1973).

The American literature offers little in respect of residential child care staff but one study concludes that the position of child care workers must be upgraded and that lack of qualified, trained child care workers represents one of the major problems confronting residential institutions (Lutheran Council in the USA, 1972).

Conclusion

The literature up to 1966 was reviewed extensively in *Residential Child Care — Facts and Fallacies* (Dinnage and Pringle, 1967). It is perhaps relevant in conclusion to see how much expansion in our knowledge about children in residential care there has been since that time and in what directions progress has been made.

Dinnage and Pringle make the point, in their review, that the main focus of research in previous years had been the effects of deprivation and institutionalization on children's development with emphasis laid upon tests of children's adjustment and achievement. They expressed the view that while the consequences of residential care for children were generally accepted as being detrimental very little was being done to find out how best to ameliorate these unfavourable consequences. Inquiry, it was felt then, should centre on questions such as: 'What should be the aim of enrichment programmes for children of different ages? In what areas of development are compensatory experiences most urgently needed? When is an individual and when a group approach appropriate? What are the role and function of remedial work? How can children best be helped to understand and come to terms with inadequate or rejecting parents? In short, how can a therapeutic community be created so that children leave residential care emotionally and intellectually strengthened, rather than even more deficient or damaged than when they entered it?'

Regrettably, little has been published in the past nine years to provide answers to these questions, despite the still urgent need. Recent research in Britain has continued to concentrate upon the consequences of residential care for children and has ignored inquiry into how these consequences might be prevented or how they might be subsequently reversed. From the literature it would appear that little attempt has been made, for example, to devise enrichment or compensatory programmes and there are no evaluative studies of such programmes where they exist. This is not the case in the United States, where much more has been done to evaluate different methods of care and treatment.

The number of children currently in care in Britain has risen steadily since 1967 yet there is a dearth of evidence concerning different types of residential care and the effects of different types of care on different types of children. Little is generally known about how the fate of these children is decided and by whom, how placement decisions are made and what factors may be taken into account before putting the child into either a large children's home, a foster home or a small family group home. And while there is considerable knowledge about the characteristics of children who remain in long-term care, few studies have examined what is being done to find alternative homes for them. What is clear, however, from the findings of Rowe and Lambert (1973) is the wide variety of practice between local authorities in relation to leaving children in long-term care or finding substitute homes. There appeared to be 'no obvious, meaningful and consistent link between unusually high and unusually low need for placement and the characteristics of the authorities or of the children in their care'.

In these respects it would appear that we have moved no great distance in our knowledge since 1966. Equally, the problems of staffing residential homes remain crucial and the general situation has not improved substantially over recent years, residential staff still tending to be looked upon as the poor relations in the field of social work. While recent reports have pointed up the need for adequate training programmes, shorter working hours and better pay, there is very little known, for example, about the attitudes of residential staff themselves and the differences in staff turnover in different types of residential settings.

In summarizing recent research findings this brief review points up the need for further research which will shed light upon some of the above questions which remain unanswered.

Implications for Policy and Practice

'. . . . The picture is not an encouraging one for those who would want the child entrusted to public care to have as nearly as possible the same opportunities as the average child will have in his own family' (Dinnage and Pringle, 1967).

In the nine years since Dinnage and Pringle wrote these words and argued the case for changes in the residential care arrangements affecting infants, young children and older children and the need for better facilities and working conditions for residential staff, very little appears to have changed either in the nature of residential care itself in this country, or, as argued in the previous section, in the findings of research which could itself inform policy and practice.

As a social phenomenon residential care for children continues, and the numbers experiencing it increase. While legislative changes appear to have inflated the number of children who are in care, there is still a real underlying increase over time even where allowance is made for these changes.

The British child care system offers a range of opportunities for substitute care for children who for whatever reason, are unable to live with biological parents. Those charged with taking decisions about the most appropriate form of care for a given child at a given time have to weigh in the balance a wide range of factors. In considering residential care, one of the difficulties is knowing for whom such care is likely to be most beneficial, and so whether it would be best for a given child to be in a residential setting. To pose the question in this form implies that there are genuine choices to be made by the individual involved in child placement, and that there is the possibility of making a choice in the light of knowledge about the consequences of various alternative courses of action.

Not only was this not the case nine years ago, it seems to have been little changed by the time of the present review. In the absence of an adequate range of resources and of knowledge about the consequences of bringing up a child in various alternative forms of substitute care, then the actual placement of any child must depend on a number of fortuitous circumstances. Patently this is no way to provide a service for children who frequently are already deprived emotionally if not physically. Of course, some forms of residential care may be entirely appropriate for some children. But we are uninformed by the literature as to which children these might be.

In terms of bringing up children in circumstances that approximate most nearly to those of a normal family, residential care would seem to offer the most costly and the least beneficial alternative. As has been pointed out above, the literature suggests little additional knowledge about residential care since the last review. As a form of provision it has in the interim been used no less, and apparently to no more effect; staff morale seems still to be low. Clearly there is a need to develop and exploit alternative forms of care which would not only be less costly in financial terms but, more important, would be less depriving to children. Therefore, it is essential that the quality of residential care should be improved for those requiring temporary assessment, for any groups who can be shown to benefit best from this provision, for children who prove beyond the capacity of alternative forms of care, i.e. as a last resort. Obviously, improvement in training status and in working conditions of staff will be essential if this is to be accomplished.

So much does the present state of knowledge reflect a similar situation to that obtaining when the earlier review was prepared, that it seems entirely appropriate to repeat here the summary and conclusions from that volume. The fact that it is by now out of print would seem an additional reason for doing so.

Conclusions and Recommendations

Reprinted from: DINNAGE, R. and PRINGLE, M.K. (1967) Residential Child Care — Facts and Fallacies (Longman)

'Effective (though not total) primary prevention of certain mental disorders is possible with what we know *now* if we but have the will to apply it ... Our nation must be prepared to invest its material substance, to an extent far beyond present conceptions, in the cultivation of people,' (Eisenberg, 1962).

To study the literature on child care is to be referred back time and time again to the social priorities which make substitute care necessary for so many children. Although the prime cause of broken families may in the majority of cases lie in parental inadequacy, it is reasonable to infer from the available evidence that this ranges from intractable pathology to an inability to cope with overwhelming circumstances. For the children of families in this latter group, the really effective services that could maintain them at home with one parent do not exist. No recommendations which ignore these deficiencies can be either forceful or honest; but the basic social provisions which could reduce the number of separated families and prevent damage to a great number of children — better housing, possibly higher Family Allowances and a special allowance enabling single parents to keep their children, a more generous policy altogether towards the sections of the community now recognized to be living well below the standards of the majority — lie outside the scope of this review. It would be a mistake, however, not to recognize that these provisions — which reflect the community's respect and concern for those handicapped by poverty or illness, childhood or old age — are the crucial determinants of whether or not children have equal chances of a basic minimum environment for healthy development.

That children in long-term substitute care do *not* generally have the same opportunities as their counterparts from the same social class who live at home, and certainly not the same opportunities as more privileged children, is clear from the research reviewed above. This is perhaps a truism to all concerned with child care work; but it is one which needs restating with some force and with factual support — for sometimes to those working most closely with children in care, to use Bowlby's phrase, 'familiarity diminishes sensitivity'.

The first step in reassessing the child care situation, therefore, is the recognition that families with a low income and several children, with only one parent, or with physical or mental handicaps, are generally at risk of disintegration; that once the family is broken and children are placed, they may acquire further handicaps, and family reintegration may be difficult; that there is an association between having been in care (among other factors) and subsequent delinquency, illegitimate pregnancies and mental illness, suggesting that pathology may be passed on to another generation (Ferguson, 1966; Barry and Lindemann, 1960; Baker and Holzworth, 1961; Earle and Earle, 1961); and that in terms of financial cost alone, it is more expensive to keep one child in care until adulthood than to provide a new home (Wynn, 1964). In the light of these facts, to make provision for special allowances for all single parents — unmarried, widowed or deserted — at risk of long separation from their children, as recommended by Wynn, and additionally to set up a special home help service for the children of these parents, would appear more than justified both in terms of cost and of humanity. That these two measures alone could effect a substantial reduction in the number of children in care, facilitating higher standards both in foster care and residential care, is suggested by the fact that mental or physical illness, desertion, or death of one parent, altogether accounted for nearly a tenth of children coming into care in 1964/5 (Children in Care in England and Wales, 1966) and that children in care for these reasons stayed there for longer than average. Both the residential and the field services in child care are facing a severe staffing crisis in the next few years (Watoon, 1964; Williams, 1967); money will have to be spent, and it seems justifiable on all counts that it should be allocated primarily towards reducing the population of children in public care, and then towards increasing the population of child care workers. Even to maintain present staffing standards will evidently require thought and effort in the future. A radical alternative to public care for some children is obviously indicated, and research is urgently needed to clarify how many children, in what type of situation, could be kept with a parent, and how successfully.

The fear is sometimes voiced — and perhaps even more frequently felt — that such measures may increase rather than reduce social problems: that higher Family Allowances will induce parents to have more children, help for unmarried mothers raise the population of illegitimate children, 'single parent' allowances or home helps perhaps encourage mothers or fathers to desert their spouses. There is no evidence that such measures introduced in other countries have had undesirable effects. A review of the outcome of these provisions, where they have been introduced, would be a valuable contribution to thinking about radical prevention.

As a small start, a home help 'demonstration project' as carried out by some American agencies could be set up (Children's Aid Society, 1962). Although the present domiciliary service is fully occupied, it is not mainly concerned with keeping children out of care; Packman (1965) found agreement among Children's Officers that on its present scale it made little difference to the child care problem. The possibility of setting up a special service linked with some training, and possibly appealing to women who are unwilling to live in residential homes, could be explored.

Provisions such as these would constitute a more radically effective preventive programme than work done piecemeal by individuals in Children's Departments. But such work within the child care services recognized officially by the Children and Young Persons Act 1963, is also important and should now be ready to progress from the stage of formal recognition to being the subject of critical examination, discussion and planning. The President of the Association of Children's Officers stated at the Annual Conference in 1961 that 'Children's Authorities have for years now regarded it as a vital part of their work to treat the family as a whole and not to deal with the child as an isolated unit'. But there is no reflection in the research and literature of how this 'vital work' is done. What proportion of time is spent on preventive work by Child Care Officers? Spent in what ways? and how successfully? Since this is always likely to be difficult and time-consuming work, research and discussion are urgently needed in order to plan it efficiently. It may be that it should be concentrated to be of maximum effectiveness — concentrated in the hands of one worker, and on selected families, rather than that many workers should spend time haphazardly with the most difficult cases. But it should be recognized that individual efforts may be hampered or even wasted unless they are carried out in the framework of genuinely preventive social measures.

Concepts like prevention (of the need for public care of children or for any other form of social first aid) commonly go through several phases: a pioneering stage when individuals work to get a new idea accepted, then a time of official recognition, and finally a stage when the details of practical implementation are thrashed out and practised (and one might add a fourth phase when complacency threatens previous achievements). Prevention has now reached the second stage, and it should be ready to enter the third. Discussion in practical, rather than theoretical, terms of its implementation at all levels should be a major inference from the findings of child care research.

To turn from recommendations for preventive provisions, to the means of improving the quality of residential care for children who cannot be kept at home by these provisions, involves a dilemma which is sometimes ignored in child care writings. No organization can function well without confidence in its value; but if substitute care, and residential care in particular, is so damaging that children must be kept out of it if at all possible – and this is now official policy – it must inevitably be hard for both field and residential staff to do their work with confidence. The knowledge that one's work involves painful experiences for children and that the care offered is inevitably second-best (second at least to their ideal parents if not the to real ones) must lead to disillusionment or denial for some workers. Even hospital staff, who have the reassurance of knowing that their work is visibly therapeutic, have found it hard to accept the findings of Bowlby and others on the emotional effects of hospitalization; while child care workers have no such assurance that – with the limited resources available at present – the care given will be therapeutic.

To stress the not very encouraging findings of many of the research reports in this book may seem to be adding to possible discouragement; but it is done in the belief that difficulties recognized are better than difficulties insidiously undermining confidence in a profession. All those giving substitute care have the task of giving the best care they can while knowing that it *is* a substitute; and perhaps the more the problem is acknowledged the less of an obstacle it may become. Residential care in particular has been depreciated in two ways: it has been considered the poorer alternative to foster care (partly as a result of research on old-fashioned orphanages and on very young children in nurseries) and it has consequently become the accepted placement for difficult children who cannot be fostered – a kind of doubly substitute care, neither own home or foster home. Whether or not the *good* foster home is always better than group care, such homes will probably always be in short supply, and the research reviewed in *Foster Home Care – Facts and Fallacies* indicates the hazards of foster home breakdown for a large number of the children cared for in families.

There is no need, therefore, for residential workers to feel that they are offering an inferior kind of care (except for very young children), but a great need for more enthusiasm about the possibilities of residential work. Research should be directed towards finding out what are the beneficial elements in group life and how they can be incorporated in homes, shifting the emphasis from (though not forgetting) what such care *cannot* be, to what it can at its best provide. There have been no studies comparing one kind of home with another, but generally research (and common sense) suggests that better and more individualized group care can affect children's adjustment considerably, and this could be explored further. Sociological analyses such as Castle's, of homes in relation to the community, would also be valuable; and the current interest in the dynamics of groups and communities could be usefully applied to children's homes. And the more children who have at least one affectionate parent and can be kept at home by preventive provisions, the easier it should be for residential staff to care confidently for a smaller population of children, who have *no* alternative home. If new confidence and professionalism can be stimulated, part of the benign circle might be a lower staff turnover.

The indefinable factor of group 'spirit' or group identification could — if it were genuine — be as valuable a counterbalance to the drawbacks of group living for the child in care as evidently it can be for the child in boarding school or kibbutz; and for the former, as for the latter, it need not conflict with family loyalty. But such group feeling would depend on the confidence and security of the adults in the group; which in turn depends on status, on community recognition, and so perhaps finally on training.

Part of this fresh attitude to residential care could be a willingness to experiment with new techniques and types of accommodation. Group discussions run by a skilled leader, for example, both for staff and for children, are described in the literature as a stimulating (and difficult) method of airing the problems of living in a community. These need not be carried out in the home; older children, especially adolescents, might benefit from attending small groups containing children from other homes or from their own families; this might serve to counteract the intellectual damping down which is evidenced in the low scholastic achievement of most children in care. Such supportive work would be facilitated if specialists were willing to lend some of their time and interest to the needs of children in care. Even one or two successful pilot projects can act as encouragement to other workers and as a counterbalance to negative attitudes towards residential care. Another experimental technique, whereby a staff member is assigned one child to observe and then discuss at meetings, is described in French papers (Appell, 1963, 1965).

New kinds of accommodation might also be further developed, isolating children less from their families and communities: sheltered accommodation for single parents and their children; weekly care for children, with weekends spent at home; special short-stay homes; homes approximating to boarding schools. Evaluation of the successes and difficulties of such schemes, where they are already being tried out, would be helpful. It is clear from the research reviewed that one of the obstacles to providing good care is the fact that some children are so damaged that no one person can tolerate their behaviour for long. By experimenting with these 'half-way houses' the burden of the more difficult children would be shared by several people and at the same time more children could remain in touch with their home backgrounds. It might also be useful, in view of Pringle's findings on the value of supportive adults outside the home, to give a new lease of life to the 'Uncle and Aunt' scheme, renaming it more appropriately and linking it with publicity and a semi-professional approach. Good-will in families who would not undertake fostering could thus be utilized. All such schemes would need to be assessed and discussed in operation and, if possible, should have a research plan 'built in' to them.

The importance of attracting and keeping good staff for residential posts scarcely needs stressing. Important points suggested by the research are the need for hours and conditions of work which stand comparison with other careers; for non-resident relief staff and domestic help; for opportunities for promotion and the recognition of seniority; and for improved communications between workers from different branches and levels of child care work. Sympathy and supervision for the new recruit during the early months are clearly of great importance; and ways might be found of maintaining the interest of young people in residential work until they are old enough to start training. Where such schemes have already operated they could be discussed and evaluated. Some research might be undertaken to compare conditions in residential child care work with other kinds of residential work, with the handicapped or in approved schools, for instance.

These are all practical recommendations; in more general terms, there are two things which emerge as supremely valuable to the child in care: continuity (as much as can possibly be available to a child separated from home), and knowledge about his background and prospects, even where this is painful. While some of the recommendations and points discussed apply only to one group among the many types of children in care, the need for these things is common to all. They are, it is true, generally recognized to be important, but it is still doubtful how far this recognition is widely expressed in practical arrangements. Some possible ways of providing continuity — by letters to children, birthday cards, presents, photographs, visits — are suggested by Lomax-Simpson (1963, 1964, 1966). The building up of files of personal letters and photographs could usefully become standard practice for long-stay children. More supportive after-care for adolescents should also receive consideration; yet Jarrett notes that few Child Care Officers in her sample considered they had time for it. There is scarcely any evidence about the difficulties of this age group, but common sense suggests that there might be a special need for supervision and support that would ease the transition from children's home to hostel and from hostel to lodgings. Permanence of staff in homes would, of course, contribute more than anything else to a sense of continuity for children at any age, but even to phase staff departures carefully should be helpful; and the importance of maintaining contacts with children's families is widely recognized.

The other important factor, knowledge of their backgrounds and histories, would in itself provide a kind of continuity for children in care. Its dissemination would depend, not only on the willingness of everyone concerned to make time to know as much as possible about the children and to talk to them, but also on the keeping of detailed and efficient records. Several authors have noted in their research the inadequacy of the case files they used.

An inquiry into methods of record-keeping and its difficulties would be useful as a preliminary to planning and getting support for an efficient system. The needs of both the child and those caring for him would have to be considered, and perhaps filed, separately. Studies of foster children suggest that there is an association between self-knowledge and good adjustment; and while there may be more children in residential than in foster care who are in touch with their families, many must need information, discussion, and the fullest chance to know 'who' they are. A study of the 'self-concept' of the child in residential care – how he sees himself in relation to his past and future and to the people in his life – similar to studies of foster children, would be illuminating.

It is common to end a review of research with recommendations for further investigations. Let it be stated here, however, that the first priority is that completed research – of which there is so often more than is realized – be carefully studied, and be *acted on.* As far as future work is concerned, prevention urgently deserves practical attention: firstly, an assessment of what is actually being done, and with what success; and secondly, an estimate of how many children are coming into care only, or mainly, for reasons other than gross parental inadequacy, and who could be maintained at home by radically prevent-measures.[1]

Secondly, the emphasis might now shift from tests of children's adjustment and achievement to practical, comparative studies of institutions of all kinds and sizes, in order to discover what kind of group works, for whom, and how. Such studies will be especially useful if the population of the Home – both adults and children – is considered as a whole, and in relation to the surrounding community. Time

---

[1] Because the prevention of unnecessary separation has been stressed, it should not be inferred that all family care is assumed to be ideal. Prevention of unfavourable factors *within* the family is outside the scope of this review but where these consist of outright cruelty or neglect, children will, of course, be removed from home as the lesser of two evils.

studies of the residential worker's day and week, similar to Burns and Sinclair's study of field staff, would be vitally useful in planning effectively the allocation of work, the stream-lining of chores and the arrangement of free time. Indeed, even the general routine of homes and the feelings of staff working there have been almost entirely neglected as subjects of research or description. The method used by some French research workers — living in and observing homes over a period of time — might produce interesting results (Recherche Sociale C.A.F., 1965; Siv, 1965). Plans for training courses, such as those advocated by the Williams Committee would be greatly facilitated if more were made known and published about daily life in residential work. Conditions might be compared with those in other types of residential work; studies of the community structure and lines of communication in different types of home would be particularly interesting. The advantages and disadvantages of small and large homes need critical evaluation; comparisons with the larger type of home favoured in some European countries (Research Department, Welfare Office, Jerusalem, 1961; Recherche Social C.A.F., 1965) might be made, and a survey of methods of training in these countries. An up-to-date study of the residential nursery and its alternatives is urgently needed.

Thirdly, future research might make some attempt to evaluate residential (and foster) placements against a background of possible alternatives and later outcome. Leonard (1957) has carried out a preliminary study of this kind. Even a limited series of longitudinal case studies, if all the relevant factors and decisions were recorded, might be very illuminating. The problem of children who come into care for short stays and remain much longer could receive special attention.

Fourthly, reports of children's own feelings about themselves and their life in care would be enlightening and would add another dimension to the research recommended above. The experiences of adolescents, both while they are still in care and afterwards, have been particularly neglected. A useful project of quite another kind would be the evaluation of the 'Aunt and Uncle' scheme as it currently exists, with proposals for replanning and extension if it appears worth while.

Fifthly, research could usefully be directed towards discovering what kind of training is most effective for those entering residential work. Even a symposium of the views of those who have taken the present courses and subsequently started work would be interesting. Also, the reasons for the high turnover of child care officers remain unexplored so far. Lastly, a survey suggests that there must be many pioneering schemes — some demanding imagination rather than money — being tried out in different areas, which do not have the benefit of even an informal description in print, let alone critical evaluation. It might be valuable if child care in this country could acquire the habit, more common in the United States, of evaluating and writing up such projects so that they could be widely discussed and perhaps adopted.

The reader who is familiar with even a proportion of the research and literature included here will realize that there is little that is new in these conclusions and recommendations. Preventive and remedial services, better conditions for residential staff, new attitudes and new techniques in group care, more continuity and more knowledge for separated children – all have been recommended before, and not only in this country. And yet it has to be concluded from a review of research results that, though child care has changed considerably over the years, there remains an uncomfortable gap between theory and practice. It may be useful, therefore, to end by considering some of the obstacles to change and improvement.

First among them are social factors which social workers are unable to control: the burden of work carried by the child care service, a burden increasing as fast as improvements are made, and the incongruity between the aims of the service and the order of social priorities which permits so many children to be dependent on public care. Secondly, although more research has been done than is perhaps recognized, there has been a lack of facilities for planning and coordinating studies and making findings widely known. There are also special pitfalls for all who work in community service, especially with children. Nokes (1960) has called attention to the danger that aims may be confused with achievements in this field, in a way which would not be possible in work which depends on visibly efficient output; and also to the fact that those who formulate the aims are seldom those who have to put them into practice. The care of children is in any case so emotional a matter, with rivalry between the different 'parents' so inevitably present, and the discrepancy often so great between the life of the child in care and what any social worker would want for his or her children, that the temptation to avoid looking at the situation as it really is must always be present. The gap between policy and actual possibilities is paralleled by the distance separating field workers and those who do the substitute parenting. These discrepancies, and the child care worker's knowledge that he is inevitably a substitute – and in the circumstances not always enabled to be a good substitute – may be responsible for the unreality which Davies (1963) describes in residential settings: the concealment of family histories and of illness and death, the inadequate provision for private life. It seems that the child care service might benefit by examining what Balbernie (1966) calls 'the authenticity of what a person or an enterprise can actually do' . . . . (*op. cit.*, pp. 23–31).

It has been said that the most difficult of all human activities is to change human attitudes. It is this and not lack of knowledge which is holding back advance. If even half of what is now clearly known were accepted with feeling and carried out with understanding by all, the picture of residential child care would be transformed. Of course, we need to know more. But meanwhile we need not, indeed cannot afford to, wait. The immediate and major problem is to will the means to translate into action what is already known. (For references in this section, see Dinnage, R. and Pringle, M.K. *Residential Child Care — Facts and Fallacies,* 1967, Longman).

Annotated
Bibliography

PART I

Research Abstracts

---

i) Who are the Children in Care?

MAPSTONE, E. (1969) 'Children in care', *CONCERN*, 3.

Scope and purpose
A study of the characteristics of a group of children who had spent some period of their lives in care.

*Sample/*314 children; all those from the 1958 Cohort of the National Child Development Study who, by the age of seven, had experienced some period in the care of a local authority or voluntary society.

*Findings/*At birth: Nearly one quarter were illegitimate. Their mothers were shorter in height and younger than mothers of the same social class whose children did not subsequently come into care. The children were more likely to have a shorter gestation period and more likely to have a lower birth weight than the rest of the cohort children.

At seven years: Children who had been in care tended to live in homes which were more crowded and had fewer facilities than other children of comparable social class who had not been in care. Nearly one half were living in households containing five or more children, compared with only 15 per cent of the cohort.

They had experienced more changes of school and were more likely to be bad attenders at school.

They did poorly as a group both in reading and in arithmetic as compared with their classmates. Proportionately three times as many as in the cohort were reported by their teachers to be poorly adjusted. Proportionately more than in the cohort were short in height and light in weight for their age.

As a group therefore these children would appear to have been at a disadvantage educationally and socially even without the additonal disturbance of reception into care.

Information on the circumstances of their care shows that 25 per cent had only one period 'in care' lasting four weeks or less while 66 per cent of the total were in care for no more than a year.

MARSDEN, G., McDERMOTT, J.F. and MINER, D. (1970) 'Residential treatment of children; a survey of institutional characteristics', *Journal of American Academy of Child Psychiatry*, 9, 2.

Describes the general characteristics of practice in 39 children's residential institutions in the United States.

The data were gathered by means of a postal questionnaire and deal with institutional characteristics such as the number of children usually in residence, the number of residential units, age limits, average length of stay, staff characteristics, parental involvement in the treatment programme and the nature of treatment provided.

Among the institutions surveyed were equal numbers of residential treatment centres and psychiatric hospital inpatient units and some differences between these two are examined. No differences were found in the numbers of children per living unit, in the acceptable age range or in willingness to accept severe forms of psychopathology. Hospitals, however, appeared less in a position to group children flexibly — either in terms of homogeneous age groups or in selected groups based on symptoms or diagnoses.

Limited comparisons are made between these findings and those of Hylton (1964).

PAPPENFORT, D.M. and KILPATRICK, D.M. (1969) 'Child-caring institutions, 1966: selected findings from the first national survey of children's residential institutions', *Social Service Review*, 43, 4.

This article presents some findings of a national survey of 2,318 public and private children's residential institutions in the United States, Puerto Rico and the Virgin Islands.

Selected information is provided in four areas: i) the history of present day institutions, ii) the problems of the children, as perceived by institution staffs, iii) services and resources available for children at the time of admission, while in residence and at the termination of care, iv) problems of institutional care and needed improvements, as reported by institution directors.

It was found that three-quarters of all children in institutions were thought by institution staffs to be emotionally disturbed. Thirteen per cent of children in institutions specifically for the emotionally disturbed were being seen regularly by psychiatrists but in other types of

institutions the proportion ranged from one per cent of those in detention to three per cent of those in homes for the dependent and neglected.

Compared with children in other types of residential care, children
in homes for the dependent and neglected were found to have the least
'psychiatric time' and the least 'casework time' available to them.

The availability of residential facilities for children is compared with
the need for them as expressed by institution directors. Shortages of
all kinds of residential facilities were reported, among them foster
homes, intensive treatment facilities, group homes, and institutions
providing temporary and emergency care only. In consequence of this
lack of resources placements were frequently felt to be less than ideal.

PINDER, R. and SHAW, M. (1974) *Summary of Research Study into
Coloured Children in Long Term Care,* University of Leicester, School
of Social Work.

Scope and purpose An exploratory study to investigate the cirum-
stances of coloured children in long-term care. It concentrates on the
background and family circumstances of the children; the situation at
the time of referral and reception into care; and the kinds of provision
made for them while in care.

Sample The study was confined to one Social Services Department in a
London borough and one large national voluntary child care agency.
From these agencies a sample of 244 children was drawn — 122 coloured
and a comparison group of 122 non-coloured.

The sample was stratified according to age at entry to care and was
restricted to children aged under five who had been in care for more
than one year, and children aged over five who had been in care for
more than two years.

Method Information was drawn from case records and from interviews
with fieldworkers, caring agents (residential staff and foster parents)
and parents. Many of the interviews were tape recorded and full trans-
cripts were made.

Findings Only a minority of the children came from what would be
regarded as normal, intact families with married parents living together.
Fewer than one child in five had been living with both parents.

The majority of coloured children were born in the UK and the great
majority of immigrant parents had been in the UK for at least two
years before the child's admission to care.

'Parental inadequacy' was seen by fieldworkers to be the reason for reception into care of one third of the children.

The child's behaviour was said to be the primary cause for admission in 16 per cent of fully coloured and seven per cent of non-coloured cases, and the immediate precipitating factor in 25 per cent of fully coloured and 11 per cent of non-coloured cases.

Police referrals were generally more common among coloured cases. Of all children in the sample just over one half were currently in compulsory care. In the borough, compulsory powers were in force for two-thirds of non-coloured and almost four-fifths of coloured children.

For non-coloured children there was generally greater use of foster homes, more placements were envisaged as long-term care and placements tended to last rather longer than for coloured children.

Contact between the fieldworker and child was often rather limited and superficial.

There appeared to be little sustained effort to keep contact or to return children to their parents; two out of three children were not expected to return home.

A substantial minority of parents of non-coloured children did not want their children back, whereas parents of coloured children were much keener for the child's rehabilitation and more resentful of current 'care'.

Only a minority of parents felt at all involved in decisions relating to the child's current life or plans for his future.

Discussion 1. It it concluded that social workers seem to operate on the basis of an image of the family which, for most children in this study, bears little relation to reality. The discrepancy between the image projected in social work ideology and the reality of every day experience is felt to be damaging to all concerned, not least to the children themselves.

2. Fieldworkers appeared to know very little about the children on their caseloads. It is questioned whether ways should be found of strengthening the child/fieldworker link or whether the balance of power should shift in favour of the adults who actually know the children (i.e. residential staff and foster parents).

ROWE, J. and LAMBERT, L. (1973) *Children Who Wait; a Study of Children Needing Substitute Families,* Association of British Adoption Agencies.

Scope and purpose A survey of children in the long-term care of local authorities and voluntary organizations, to investigate how many were in need of permanent substitute parents, what these children were like, what sort of homes were most needed and why they had not already been placed. Besides statistical information regarding the children there is a descriptive account of the foster and adoption services in the participating agencies.

Sample 2,812 children in 33 voluntary and statutory agencies through-out England, Scotland and Wales. All the children had been in care for at least six months and were under the age of 11.

On the basis of variety in size and type of both local authorities and voluntary societies eight local authorities in Scotland, 20 in England and Wales and five voluntary child care societies were selected to pro-vide an adequate and balanced picture of the national situation. The 28 local authorities included 12 counties, 12 county boroughs and four London boroughs.

In each local authority and voluntary society a sufficient number of area teams were included to produce between 70-100 children.

Method Children of the right age and length of stay in care were identi-fied from index record cards. A three part questionnaire for each child was completed in turn by a member of the administrative staff, the social worker and one of the project readers. Descriptive data about the structure, policies and home finding methods of each agency were gathered by a senior social worker.

The information was tabulated by computer. No formal tests for statistical significance were used on the results.

The main findings 1. Need for placement. Twenty-two per cent of the study children were thought by their social workers to need a sub-stitute family.

2. Childen who needed families.

i) Two out of three were boys, a similar proportion was of school age and less than 10 per cent under two-years-old. Twenty-six per cent were fully or partly of West Indian, Asian or African background.

ii) More than half the children needing placement were living with siblings for whom homes were also required.

iii) One in three exhibited behaviour problems, and more than one in five was thought to be below average in intelligence. The child's present health gave cause for concern in 18 per cent of cases and for 14 per cent of the children there was believed to be a risk of inherited illness or defect.

iv) Children who needed placement had much less family contact than those for whom continued residential care was the planned choice.

3. Type of facilities needed. Permanent substitute families were

being sought for nearly three-quarters of the children needing placement.
4. Obstacles to placement as seen by the children's social worker.
Most frequently mentioned was the problem of finding homes for
sibling groups.
5. Homefinding services. In most agencies the main problem in
homefinding was pressure of other work.
6. Information about children in long-term care. Two distinct categories of children emerged from the study:

i) Single illegitimate children who tended to come into care as babies,
have little contact with parents, and stay a very long time unless
adopted.
b) Sibling groups from disorganized families, who came in and out of
care more often, had more contact with parents and were less likely
to remain in care throughout their childhood.

Implications for practice. Short-term
i) Planning for priorities and allocation of resources is inhibited
by the lack of statistics on how many children need new parents.
ii) There should be a greater commitment on the part of staff to get
children placed. More people will come forward for older and difficult
children provided their needs are made known and adequate social
work services are made available.
iii) Better liaison with other professions could provide additional
resources for successful family placement. More use could be made
of assessment by psychologist and psychiatrists. Inter-agency placements should become more widespread.

Long-term
iv) Children who have been deprived often need compensatory
experiences in care. These may include remedial education, opportunities to learn new skills, medical attention and psychotherapy as
well as the chance to make relationships with dependable adults.
v) Better psychosocial diagnosis of the families of children coming
into care is required if earlier decisions are to be made and more effective plans put into motion. There is a need for a scale or framework
against which parenting capacity can be measured.

SCHAFFER, H.R. and SCHAFFER, E.B. (1968) *Child Care and the
Family; a Study of Short-term Admission to Care,* Bell.

Scope and purpose A comparative study of the characteristics of two
groups of families who when faced with the same crisis situation —
namely the mother's temporary incapacity to care for her children on

account of her confinement in hospital — made different arrangements for the substitute care of their children. It sets out to investigate why some families are able to make private arrangements for their children's care during this period while others place their children in the care of the local authority.

Sample One hundred families whose children were taken into care during their mothers confinement in hospital (referred to as the child care group) and 100 families who made private arrangements for their children's care (the control group). The investigation took place in a large burgh in the industrial lowlands of Scotland — an area with considerable housing and economic problems.

Method The names of the child care cases were obtained from the admissions book of the Health and Welfare Department over a period of 11 months in 1965/66. Mothers were interviewed subsequent to their admission to hospital and on each occasion a child care mother was interviewed, a control was selected from the other mothers in the same ward. Selection was random apart from two stipulations (a) the control mother was to have at least one older child who had not been received into care on this occasion and (b) was to belong to the same socioeconomic class as the child care mother.

Information was collected by interview schedules and was supplemented by reports submitted on each family by health visitors after the mother had been discharged.

The findings were grouped under the following headings:
  1. Demographic and ecological characteristics of the families.
  2. Arrangements made for the children's care.
  3. Relationships with the extended family.
  4. Families and the community.
  5. Parents and their children.

Conclusion The basic conclusion of the inquiry is seen to be that it is not so much the existence of 'real' 'objective' difficulties that account for a family's decision to send its children into care as the extent to which interpersonal relationships are valued and fostered in that family and used as a means of providing security. Thus the application for care was rarely the result of just temporary practical difficulties encountered by an otherwise satisfactorily functioning family: more often it signified a more fundamental weakness of family life expressed in such diverse ways as poor community integration, rigid conjugal role segregation, lack of supportive contact with kin, and high incidence of separations in the children.

Immediate preventive action — in the sense of making more desirable arrangements for children than admission to short-term care — should be dealt with as a routine part of antenatal care. The mother's admission to hospital should be planned as a family event requiring a multi-service approach and inquiries regarding their plans for their older children should be made of all mothers who are due for a hospital confinement.

SHAPIRO, P.C. (1968a) 'Illegitimacy and child care', *New Society*, 11, 277.

This article describes a small study designed to determine the proportion of long-term illegitimate children to all long-term children in care.

Sample Seven Children's Officers were approached and asked to provide information on the numbers of illegitimate children in care. The case records of 100 illegitimate children in the care of one Children's Department were examined.

Findings
1. Eighty-six per cent of the children had been under the age of five when first admitted to care: Fifty per cent under the age of one year and 20 per cent were less than one-month-old.
2. The two most important factors in reasons for their admission were abandonment by the mother and the mother's mental incapacity. Fifty-four per cent of children were accounted for under these two categories.
3. The children had been in care for periods ranging from three to eighteen years.
4. As regards the putative fathers the general impression was one of evasion of all responsibility. No information at all was available for 35 fathers and many had gone to other parts of the country or the world. Only seven were showing any interest in the child.

Conclusion In the light of her findings from this limited investigation the author stresses the need for more research in this field which could answer questions such as — are we doing enough to help newly arrived immigrants? are we providing adequate family planning services and are they reaching those people most in need? what kind of services are available to unmarried mothers, both for those wishing to keep their babies and for others who seek adoption for them?

SHAPIRO, P. (1968b) 'Some illegitimate coloured children in long-term care', *Case Conference*, 15, 1.

A comparative study of 35 coloured and 65 white illegitimate children in long-term care.

Sample A random sample of 100 illegitimate children who had been in the care of a large city's Children's Department for more than two years. Thirty-five children were coloured.

In all, 56 children were fathered by immigrants or temporary residents in this country; the mothers were predominantly indigenous.

The size of the sample means that statistically significant results cannot be provided.

Findings Fifty-one per cent of coloured children had been deserted by their mothers compared with 26 per cent of the 65 white children.

Ninety-four per cent of coloured children were aged under five on admission to care compared with 81 per cent of the other group.

Fifty-four per cent of coloured children were aged under one year on admission to care compared with 47 per cent of white children.

In the group of coloured children only three mothers were in contact with their children but six of the coloured putative fathers were showing interest, compared with only one father in the white group.

Forty-three per cent of coloured children were fostered compared with 37 per cent of white children. Seven coloured children were transferred to voluntary homes compared with three white children. In other respects the care offered the two groups of children appeared similar.

Conclusion The impression gained from this study, by the author, is one of immigrant fathers and unstable mothers in often brief associations. It is felt that further research may substantiate a belief that more contact with immigrant fathers may be the best means of helping these coloured illegitimate children in care to a happier self-identity.

WALTON, R.G. and HEYWOOD, M.C. (1971) *The Forgotten Children: a Study of Children in Care,* University of Manchester, Department of Extra Mural Studies.

Scope and purpose A survey of children in care, in order to give an up-to-date picture of the reasons for admission and the type of care provided by Children's Departments.

Sample Three hundred and sixty-seven children who were 'in care' at 31st March, 1969, taken from 13 local authority Children's Departments in and around Manchester.

Method Pre-coded questionnaires were completed for each Department. The information was extracted from departmental case files, admission and discharge registers and from records of parental contributions. The data — essentially descriptive — were analysed by computer; over 60 tables of comparison from the basis of the report. In some cases results are compared with information from the Government Social Survey of 1956.

Findings 1. Reasons for admission to care. Ten per cent of children in the sample had been admitted because of having no parent or guardian, being abandoned or lost, or on account of their mother's death. Thirteen per cent were in care following their mother's desertion. Parental long-term illness, particularly mental illness, was the reason for 12 per cent of admissions. Thirty-seven per cent of the children had been committed to care under a Fit Person Order.

2. Length of stay in care. The proportion of children who had been in care for ten years or more was 13.5 per cent in 1969 compared with 11.7 per cent in 1956.

3. The children and their background. The proportion of illegitimate children was 33 per cent, and of handicapped 16.6 per cent. One-sixth of the children were coloured or half-caste.

The children came from families characterized by low social class, a high proportion of fathers who were unemployed or irregular workers, and low family income.

Just under one-third of the children had been in care once or more previously and nearly a half had had no contact with their parents during the preceding six months.

Recommendations It is recommended that local authority Health Departments and Social Services Departments should work together more closely in developing family planning and abortion services and in providing supportive services for mothers bringing up a family alone.

— That stronger links be developed with the Department of Employment to ensure comprehensive planning for training and rehabilitation services for unemployed or irregular workers.
— That the possibility of putting fostering resources on a regional level should be examined and that the provision of more specialist appointments to develop these resources should be encouraged.

— That extended training programmes should be provided to improve
the skills of residential staff.

— That local authority Social Services Departments should develop
their own small scale research with projects linked to operational and
planning needs.

WEINTROB, A (1974) 'Changing population in adolescent residential
treatment; new problems for program and staff', *American Journal
Orthopsychiatry*, 44, 4.

This article documents a study to test the hypothesis that the population of an adolescent treatment centre was changing significantly in the
direction of more severe disturbance.

The population of the Centre for the years 1969-1972 was studied
and admissions and discharges in each year were compared. The exact
number of young people who passed through the Centre during the
study period is not recorded, but the Centre is said to have a population
of 40 residents (20 boys and 20 girls).

It was found that psychiatric hospitals had become the major referral
source and that the major diagnostic category had shifted from personality disorders to schizophrenic. Statistically significant changes were
also found in — prior hospital experience, the frequency of hospitalization during placement, the use of medication and the need for psychiatric treatment. It is suggested that similar changes are occurring throughout the United States in most residential treatment units.

Possible causal factors are discussed, as well as the implications of
these findings for staff and treatment programmes.

It is suggested that existing programmes are no longer adequate and
that vocational, therapeutic and educational programmes must be
altered so that they will be more consistent with the needs of the more
disturbed young people. It is also recommended that plans be made for
continued care in the form of financial aid, psychotherapy, casework
and hostel provision.

ii) The Consequences of Residential Care for Children

BROWN, J. and SOLOMON, D. (1974) 'Leisure time interest of children in residential homes', *Residential Social Work*, 14, 8.

This paper describes a pilot project, undertaken by social work students
at Manchester University, to explore the leisure time interests of a group

of children in residential care.

Sample A randomly selected sample of 44 children and young people (aged 11 to 16 years) who had been in care for at least six months and who came from 16 different homes — including family group homes, larger community homes, a boys-only home and a home for maladjusted children.

Method Thirty-seven children were interviewed by social work students using a questionnaire which incorporated both open and closed questions. From a general survey of the replies, an impression of leisure time interests of a child in a residential home was obtained.

Findings Boredom among the children was serious and most said they were frequently bored or fed up.

A few of the children had individual interests — for example, fishing, drawing, but these 'were most exceptional'; rarely did the children have a personal collection (e.g. stamps) or make or create things on their own in the children's home.

Few children named friends outside the home; some said they did not have a friend.

Conclusion Despite increasing emphasis in recent years on extending and widening leisure time experiences for young people, it is felt that 'the children's home is as yet the most neglected area when it comes to considering a leisure time policy'. Social Services Departments are urged to look beyond the essential feeding and clothing needs of the children in their care and direct their attention to the quality of life in their caring institutions.

CHEYNE, W.M. and JAHODA, G. (1971) 'Emotional sensitivity and intelligence in children from orphanages and normal homes', *Journal of Child Psychology and Psychiatry*, 12, 2.

Scope and purpose A group of children brought up in orphanages in Glasgow was compared for emotional sensitivity with a matched group of children from normal homes.

Sample Eighty children from two orphanages and 80 children from normal homes. Eight children of each sex of six-, seven-, eight-, nine- and ten-years-old were grouped and each subgroup matched for non-verbal intelligence and socioeconomic status. The samples were predominantly children of unskilled manual workers.

Method Each child was tested individually for vocabulary, non-verbal intelligence and emotional sensitivity.

Emotional sensitivity was tested using 16 voice recordings selected according to three variables: 1) Emotion (anger; happiness; love; sadness), 2) Sex of speaker, 3) Speech of speaker (educated/uneducated). Picture cards portraying the four emotions were also used.

Findings 1. Total emotional sensitivity scores. There were no significant differences in overall sensitivity between groups with different home backgrounds, nor between sexes.

2. Comparison of different emotions. There was significant variance between emotions and this was found to interact with age but not with any other of the subject variables. Positive emotions were less easily identified than negative ones.

3. Sex and speech of speakers. Emotions in female voices were more easily recognized by all children than in male voices and in educated voices more easily than in uneducated voices.

4. Recognition scores correlated with both verbal and non-verbal ability and correlations decreased with age.

Conclusion There was no clear-cut deficiency in emotional sensitivity in the orphanage children compared with children from normal homes. It seems that though an orphanage background may affect emotional sensitivity in an indirect fashion by affecting experience with different kinds of speakers, or by affecting the development of verbal ability, the evidence does not suggest that differences can be attributed to differences in emotional background. It is concluded that the development of emotional sensitivity is related more to general perceptual and intellectual factors than to specific experience with emotions.

DAVIS, N. and HEIMLER, E. (1967) 'An experiment in the assessment of social function', *The Medical Officer*, 117, 3.

A small pilot study was undertaken to assess and analyse areas of satisfaction and frustration in a sample of adults brought up in Dr Barnardo's Homes, and the results were compared with those obtained from samples from various agencies (Family Service Units, Mental Health Departments and the Probation Service) and from the community at large.

A new instrument — the Heimler Scale of Social Function — was used to assess five particular areas: finance, sex, primary and secondary family relationships, friendship, work and/or outside interests.

It was found that the Dr Barnardo's sample scored lowest in the

Primary Family area but the Secondary Family score was higher for Dr Barnardo's than for the agency samples, although considerably less than the non-agency samples. Sexually they scored very much within the normal range but their 'friendship' score was down compared with non-agency samples. It also appeared that they derived less satisfaction from their work and outside interests than the non-agency samples. Statistically significant conclusions could not be drawn in view of the size of the samples.

FRANCIS, S.H. (1971) 'The effects of own-home and institution-rearing on the behavioural development of normal and mongol children', *Journal of Child Psychology and Psychiatry*, 12, 3.

Scope and purpose The purposes of this study were 1) to outline briefly the pattern of development of play behaviour, in a familiar environment, by normal and mongol children and 2) to use this outline of development as a basis on which to compare the effects of home and institution rearing on this behaviour.

The effects of institution rearing on mongol and normal children are compared.

Sample Four groups of children distributed according to chronological age and development level.

1. Children diagnosed at birth as mongols, with a mental age of two years and less and chronologically below four years — a) Home-reared and b) Institution-reared.

2. Children under two-years-old, regarded as normal at birth — a) Home-reared and b) Institution-reared.

Method Observations of the children at play were made by the author. Recording was not started until the children began playing without paying undue attention to the observer. Various types of behaviour were recorded, these were grouped under — diffuse movements, self-oriented behaviours, postures, object oriented behaviour, movement and visual attention.

The children's development level was assessed using a test developed by Woodward (1959). Each child was assigned to one of six stages for which approximate mental ages are given.

Findings 1. Normal and mongol development. Half the behaviours considered showed no difference between the normal and mongol children, underlining the basic similarity in behavioural development in these two groups. What differences there were suggested that at all developmental levels the normal children were more alert and active than mongols.

2. Effect of institution-rearing upon normal and mongol development and behaviour. Institution-reared normal and mongol children were behaviourally more retarded than their home-reared counterparts of the same chronological age, and the institution-reared mongols were significantly retarded developmentally.

Developmental retardation of institution-reared normal children has been widely reported but was not found in this study.

The retardation of the normal children was less marked than among mongol children.

The institution children's behaviour was characterized by a higher incidence of less mature behaviours and a lower incidence of the more organized, advanced behaviours like locomotion and constructive play, than were found for home-reared children.

Conclusion It is suggested that the institution environment is an important factor in producing developmental and behavioural retardation. The institution mongols had fewer toys available, were more likely to be restrained and, except when able to walk, experienced less social contact than home mongols; the institution normal children received less social contact than the home normal children, except when able to walk. The paucity of toys available to the institution mongols might account for their small amount of object oriented play and retarded sensorimotor development.

Although the institution reared normal children had good supplies of toys they also showed less object-oriented behaviour and less visual attention to objects than did home-reared normal children when compared on the basis of developmental level, and they were more retarded in their sensorimotor development.

HARRIS, D. (1973) 'Television and the child in residential care', *Community Schools Gazette*, 67, 8.

In order to see how residential establishments for children and young people approach their parenting responsibilities with regard to television the author spoke to the people in charge of six establishments — a Reception Centre, a Family Group Home, a Boys' Remand Home, a Probation Hostel and two Community Schools for Boys. It was found that the extent to which television is used and how it is used varies between different establishments and their residents and staff, but there was a general impression that the importance of television to the children is not as great as some commentators would fear.

KEYTE, M. (1974) 'Caring: the point of view of 28 children and some of their parents', *Social Work Today*, 5, 1.

This article reports a small survey of the residential experience of children in long-term care. It examines aspects of the residential care situation as revealed by interviews with 28 children from four different establishments, and with some of their parents.

The study sets out to answer such questions as − How far do children living in residential homes maintain contact with the local community? Does this differ between homes? How much is group living geared to the needs of the children and how much to routine? Where do parents fit in? What do they know about where their child is going when he leaves home? Are they able to discuss his subsequent progress? How much does the child communicate of his experiences away from the family?

Method A comparison was made of four establishments, two of which were for 'family groups' and two for more than 20 children each. The ages of the children ranged from seven to seventeen years and their length of stay in the home ranged from eight months to seven years − the average being three years.

Separate questionnaires were devised for children and parents and these were administered during individual interviews. The children's questionnaire touched on items such as school, food, clothes, interests, friends, holidays, staff and contact with parents and siblings.

Ten sets of parents were interviewed, 'to obtain their impressions of establishment and also to examine how much they feel involved in their child's way of life when he is separated from them'. The questionnaire covered such areas as information given about the home, current contact, home visits and communication of the child's experiences.

Findings There were marked differences in the response to questions from children placed in different establishments. In the first family group home where the children were younger they appeared to be 'home oriented' in contrast to the older group in the second family group home who showed a preference for peer group activities. In the large homes the degree of contact with the local community seemed more a matter of staff attitude.

Regarding comments about staff and family contact, there was no apparent difference between the establishments. Just over half the children expressed a preference for talking to a particular member of staff about important issues and half of these thought he or she was always available.

Fourteen of the children were in regular contact with their parents and half of those admitted to some degree of upset after visits or telephone contact.

Findings regarding the parents showed that their knowledge of their children's way of life, daily routine, interests and contacts varied considerably. More than half had not been told about the establishment before the child was placed there, and although residential staff were thought to be readily available to parents, only four were satisfied with the information given about their children. There was no apparent difference between the establishments; in general, the parents were 'bewildered about lack of real contact with residential social workers'.

It is concluded that more thought is required about the effects of separation upon the parents. Lack of communication between social workers and parents can only enhance the latter's anxiety; the author feels that it would be helpful to clarify the roles of field and residential staff in this respect.

KOHEN-RAZ, R. (1968) 'Mental and motor development of kibbutz, institutionalized and home-reared infants in Israel', *Child Development,* 39, 2.

A study of the mental and motor development of kibbutz infants compared with that of a group of institutionalized children and a group of children living in private middle class homes.

Sample One hundred and thirty kibbutz babies drawn from the total population of infants available at the 21 kibbutzim selected as representative of all kibbutz settlements in the country.

One hundred and fifty-two babies from private homes in Jerusalem and Rehovet, where either mother or father had at least completed high school.

Seventy-nine babies selected from the total population in five baby homes in Jerusalem, Tel Aviv and Haifa.

All the children were aged between one to twenty-seven months, had been born in Israel and had remained in the country continuously. No parent had immigrated after 1960 and at least one parent of each child was Jewish.

With respect to parental ethnic origin there were no essential differences between the private home and kibbutz samples. The majority of the institution babies were assumed to originate from the lower socioeconomic strata of the Israeli population.

Method The Bayley Infant Scales of Mental and Motor Development were administered by five female examiners with the participation of the mothers or caretakers of the children. A standard interview questionnaire was administered to mother and caretaker and detailed information regarding the baby's daily routine and habits were recorded.

Findings 1. *Mental Development.* Compared with an American sample the kibbutz and private home babies showed consistently higher overall achievements on the Mental Scale.

Kibbutz infants were found to show consistent superiority over the Israeli private-home infants at the lower age groups but achievements of both groups became practically equal until after 12 months when the kibbutz babies tended to perform inconsistently lower.

The institutionalized babies showed a conspicuous retardation when compared with the other Israeili groups.

Mothers education and preference for outside work were positively related to the mental level of male infants in the private home sample.

2. *Motor Development.* The kibbutz and private home infants were equal on the Motor Scales compared with the American sample.

Institutionalized infants were found to be motorically retarded up to the age of 15 months but from 18-27 months performed at an equal level with kibbutz and private home babies.

Eye-hand coordination and walking appeared relatively less variable cross-culturally than capacity to recover hidden objects, language functions, keeping body equilibrium and fine motor coordination.

Conclusion The findings suggest that collective education in the kibbutz does not have an adverse effect on the mental and motor development of infants. The evident contrast between the precocity of the kibbutz infants and the retardation of institutionalized babies does not seem to justify previous attempts to find close similarity between methods of infant care in institutions and in collective education.

ROSEN, A.C. (1971a) 'Are children in children's homes overprotected?', *Child in Care*, 11, 2.

Sample Thirty-three houseparents from various children's homes run by Dr Barnardo's were asked whether they considered children in children's homes to be 'overprotected'. Twenty-five of the houseparents were in charge of separate cottages in a large cottage community and eight were from smaller homes.

Findings All 33 respondents regarded children in contemporary children's homes as 'overprotected'.

The examples given fell under two main headings: 1. Restriction of the child's freedom of movement outside the children's home. 2. Automatic provision for a meeting of all the child's material needs.

Discussion A major aim of contemporary residential child care is to provide the child with an environment as like to that of a normal home as possible. However, a major effect of the examples of overprotection cited by the respondents is to set the child in care *apart* from other children. A further effect is that when a teenager leaves a children's home after many years in care he or she is scarcely likely to be well prepared for an independent life in the outside world.

ROSEN, A.C. (1971b) 'The social and emotional development of children in long-term residential care', *Therapeutic Education,* Spring.

Scope and purpose A study of children in long-term residential care to determine the effects of being depriv   of a normal family life on their social, emotional, intellectual and educational development. This paper focuses attention on social and emotional development only.

Sample 1. Twenty, eight- to nine-year-olds (ten boys and ten girls)
          Twenty 13- to 14-year-olds (ten boys and ten girls)
Selected at random from a cottage community of over 200 children, run by Dr Barnardo's.
          2. Nineteen, eight- to nine-year-olds (13 boys and six girls).
          Nineteen 13- to 14-year-olds (13 boys and six girls)
Selected from a number of smaller homes for between 15-31 children, also run by Dr Barnardo's.
          Any children receiving special educational treatment were excluded. All the children had been in the homes for at least six months.

Method To investigate the personal autonomy or self-direction of the child, each child was given the self-direction subscales of the Manchester Scales of Social Adaption (Lunzer, 1966). Results were compared with those of children not in care (from published norms).

Findings 1. *Social Development.* Eight- to nine-year-olds in residential care scored similarly to eight- to nine-year-olds living in their own homes, but 13- to 14-year-olds in residential care were very much retarded in personal independence as compared with children living at home.
          Children in care had less freedom of movement, were more closely supervised and were less adept in money matters than children living in their own homes.

2. *Emotional Development.* To investigate adjustment, a Child Scale 'A' (Rutter, 1970) was completed for each child by the houseparents in charge.

Eighteen per cent of eight- to nine-year-olds and 19 per cent of 13- to 14-year-olds were found to be maladjusted (as estimated from the Child Scale 'A' scores). At both age levels this is considerably higher than Rutter *et al.'s* figures for the child population at large, *viz.* six per cent. The bulk of the maladjusted children in this study — both boys and girls — were characterized by antisocial disorders (stealing, destroying other people's property, disobedience, etc.) rather than neurotic disorders (sleep difficulties, often worried, etc.). This is in contrast to findings for the child population at large where there is a marked sex difference in the distribution of antisocial as opposed to neurotic disorders, proportionately more boys being antisocial than girls.

STEELE, C.I. (1971) 'Sexual identity problems among adolescent girls in institutional placement', *Adolescence*, 6, 24.

Scope and purpose A study designed to determine if girls placed in an institutional setting during adolescence differed in the process of establishing an appopriate sexual identity from girls who had continued to live in their parental homes with their biological mothers.

Sample Thirty-six girls aged 15-17 years who had been removed from their biological mothers during early adolescence and who were living in an institution, and a control group of thirty-six girls aged 15-17 who were living with their biological mothers. The institution group excluded girls whose reasons for placement were severe delinquent behaviour, illegitimate pregnancy or psychiatric disorders needing treatment.

Method Measurements of conscious and unconscious femininity were selected. The subjects were tested on the Gough Femininity Scale, the Femininity Scale of the Strong Vocational Interest Blank for Women, and an adaptation of Murray's Thematic Apperception Test.

Findings Data showed that the 'placed' girls as a group scored consistently lower than did the 'non-placed' girls on all measures of femininity.

Problems in sexual identification and ego identity tended to be extended into later adolescence among the placed subjects, while girls living with their biological mothers expressed fewer and less severe problems in these areas and tended toward attenuation of such difficulties at an earlier age.

It is suggested that low scores on measures of femininity among adolescent girls can serve to alert therapists and other professionals to the fact that these girls may require special help with potentially serious problems in sexual identification.

TIZARD, B. and JOSEPH, A. (1970) 'Cognitive development of young children in residential care. A study of children aged 24 months', *Journal of Child Psychology and Psychiatry,* 11, 3.

Scope and purpose A study planned to assess the effectiveness of changes made in residential nurseries — such as the introduction of small mixed age groups, increased staffing and the attachment of particular staff to particular groups of children — in preventing retardation in young children growing up in long-stay residential nurseries. A group of institutional children were compared at two years with a group of children matched for age and sex in working class families in London.

Sample Fifteen boys and girls, approaching the age of two, in the care of three large voluntary societies. They were selected as having been healthy full-term babies with no birth complications, who had had no subsequent illness and who had entered a residential nursery in good health before the age of four months and had not been subsequently moved. Five boys and five girls were coloured.

The cognitive development of this group was compared with thirty working class children living at home in London. The control group was in no sense a sample but was considered illustrative of small well-functioning London working class families. Two of the fathers were unemployed, the rest were either skilled, semi-skilled or unskilled workers. One-third of the group were 'only' children.

Method 1. Before testing, the children's fear of strangers and response to separation were rated in a standardized situation.

2. Test Procedure. The Cattell Infant Intelligence Scale — containing verbal and non-verbal items was used. Verbal and non-verbal scores were calculated by giving a score of one to each subtest passed, beginning at the 12 month level.

3. Some assessment of the child's spontaneous language and of certain everyday experiences was also made.

Findings 1. Children living at home were significantly more friendly than the nursery children.

2. Using the Cattell Infant Intelligence Test Scales, no significant differences were found between the scores of boys and girls in either

the home or the nursery group, or between the coloured and the white children in the nursery.
The mean mental age of the nursery children was two months behind the norm.
Most of the difference between the groups was in verbal scores but there was also a small significant difference in non-verbal scores.
Twenty per cent of nursery children had no verbal successes above the 20 month level; none of the home children had such poorly developed language.
3. Home children vocalized much more than nursery children and used a larger vocabulary.
4. The mean score of the nursery children for play experience was higher, but not significantly so, than that of the home children. Nursery children had significantly fewer neighbourhood social experiences and significantly fewer experiences of the adult world.

Discussion Despite great improvements made in recent years, the residential nursery considered as a language laboratory appears inferior to a 'good' working class home. Three aspects of the nursery environment may contribute to this inferiority. Firstly the adult/child ratio in all but the best staffed nurseries provides less opportunity for the children to communicate with adults. Secondly, limitation of experience of the outside world might be expected to narrow the children's vocabulary, and thirdly, language development may be affected by the fact that staff and child relationships may be too casual to encourage communication.
It is noted that no necessary implications for later development can be drawn from a study of two-year-olds.

TIZARD, J. and TIZARD, B. (1971) 'The social development of two-year-old children in residential nurseries'. In: SCHAFFER, H.R. (ed) *The Origins of Human Social Relations*, New York, Academic Press.

Scope and purpose The report of one of a series of studies into the development of young children in different types of residential care. Two-year-old children being reared in long-stay residential nurseries are compared with working class two-year-old children being brought up in their own homes by both parents in a relatively favourable environment in which the mother is not working full-time and in which there are no older children of pre-school age.

Sample Fifteen boys and fifteen girls who had entered a residential nursery in good health before the age of four months and had not subsequently been moved. All but one of the children were illegitimate; five boys and five girls were coloured.

The control group consisted of 15 boys and 15 girls approaching the age of two who had been healthy full-term babies and had not subsequently been hospitalized.

Method All the children were observed in their own living room, with their mother or most familiar nurse present, and were assessed by one experimenter for response to strangers, response to separation and attachments. Inquiries were made about number of caretakers, number of adult contacts, number of child contacts and emotional behaviour patterns.

Conclusion The development of the nursery children differed from that of home reared children in certain respects notably in their relationships with their caretakers and with strangers. Nursery children were less willing to approach or to stay alone with strangers and with familiar adults (in certain situations) they were more clinging. Despite attempts by the nurseries to approximate to family life differences between them and real families are so numerous that a variety of possible explanations for the typical behaviour of nursery children can be advanced. Among the differences measured in this study were the lack of neighbourhood experiences of nursery children, the multiplicity of their caretakers and peer contacts and the more limited emotional involvement of caretakers.

It is suggested that the children's relationships with one another and with adults change as they get older, and that the nature of this social relationship depends on the specific manner in which residential care is organized rather than on 'institutional' care as such.

WOLKIND, S.N. (1974a) 'Sex differences in the aetiology of antisocial disorders in children in long-term residential care', *British Journal of Psychiatry*, 125, August.

Scope and purpose A psychiatric study of the factors which are related to the development of antisocial disorder in boys and girls in a long-stay children's home.

Sample Ninety-two children (39 girls, 53 boys) aged between five and 12 years who had been resident in a large children's home for at least six months. The children were housed in cottages of 15-20 children.

Method The child and his or her houseparents were interviewed; the results of these two interviews were combined and a clinical diagnosis made. If the child was felt to show psychiatric disturbance a severity rating of mild or severe was made depending on the degree of handicap caused by the symptoms. Case notes were used to gather information about the child's background, family and experiences of being in care.

Fifty-four of the children had spent over half of their lives in care, 30 had had only one admission to care and a further 30 had had four or more separate admissions. The most common reasons for admission to care were — mother unable to cope; desertion by the mother; or cruelty by the parents.

Findings Forty per cent of the boys and 26 per cent of the girls were shown to have an antisocial or mixed antisocial/neurotic disorder.

Examination of the factors related to the development of antisocial disorder suggests that for boys who have experienced either brief or prolonged periods in care, both the reception into care and the antisocial disorder are secondary to factors in the boy's family. Lack of contact with a father and large family size were both found to relate significantly to antisocial disorder in boys, but not in girls. Early admission to an institution does not appear to be an aetiological factor in antisocial disorder in boys but for girls there was found a positive relationship between prolonged early experience of residential care and antisocial disorder. Among the girls there was no apparent association between deviant family structure and antisocial disorder.

WOLKIND, S.N. (1974b) 'The components of "affectionless psychopathy" in institutionalized children', *Journal of Child Psychology and Psychiatry*, 15, 3.

Scope and purpose A psychiatric study of a group of children in a long-stay institution which examines the relationships between some features of 'affectionless psychopathy' and factors in the child's family and experience.

Sample Ninety-two children aged five to 12 years who had been resident in a large children's home for at least six months. They came from a socially deprived area and from a background of extreme family disorganization. Fifty-four of the children had spent over one half of their lives in care. Thirty children had had only one admission to care and a further 30 had had four or more separate admissions.

Method Each child and later the child's houseparents were interviewed using standardized interviews. The results of the two interviews were combined and a clinical diagnosis made. Information about the child's background, family and experience of being in care was collected from case notes.

Findings Sixty-nine children were diagnosed as having a psychiatric disorder; in 36 children this was a neurotic disorder and in 24 cases an antisocial disorder.

A rating of disinhibition was given far more frequently for children admitted to care before the age of two, than for those not admitted until after that age.

Antisocial disorder was found to be associated with an intermittently or permanently absent father, and with large family size.

Conclusion The findings suggest that the main features of the 'affectionless psychopathy' syndrome have a different aetiology. Antisocial disorder was found to relate to aspects in the child's family; relationship difficulties were associated with an early admission to care, disinhibition for example, being almost confined to children admitted before the age of two.

The implications are that to attempt at all costs to keep a child with its own family would not be the way to prevent the development of psychiatric disorders as many children appear to be severely damaged by their experiences prior to the admission. Attempts must be made to identify the factors within the children's home which are likely to cause further damage to the child after its admission.

WOLKIND, S. and RUTTER, M. (1973) 'Children who have been "In Care" — an epidemiological study', *Journal of Child Psychology and Psychiatry*, 14, 2.

Scope and purpose An examination of the psychiatric state and family circumstances of children admitted into short-term care compared with other groups of children who had not experienced residential care.

Sample On the Isle of Wight in 1969 and in an Inner London Borough in 1970 all children in the 10-11 year age group were screened by use of teachers' questionnaires for behaviour problems in the classroom. In each case a group of children was selected as showing difficulties and a randomly selected control group was more intensively studied. In all 1,278 children living on the Isle of Wight and 1,689 children living in an Inner London borough were included in the study.

Method Parents of the selected children were interviewed and information obtained about the family and the parental relationship. Details of all the child's separations from the parents were obtained and any reception into local authority care was recorded if it lasted for as long as one week. Further information on the child's behaviour, emotions and relationships was obtained and on this basis a diagnosis of psychiatric disorder was made, according to tested criteria.

Findings In both communities there was a strong and statistically significant association between a period 'in care' and behavioural disturbance as shown both at home and at school. This association was much more marked for boys than for girls.

Over one in six of the children diagnosed as having a psychiatric disorder had been in care; a rate which differed significantly from that of the control groups.

Information on the children's family circumstances after leaving care showed that 67 per cent were living in a family of four or more children (compared with 39 per cent of control children) and less than one in four were living in families where the parents were rated as having a harmonious marital relationship (compared with nearly two-thirds of control children).

The findings suggest that children experiencing short-term institutional care are 'at risk' of antisocial disorder, not so much because of the effects of the care *per se* but rather because such children are liable to come from disturbed families. It is suggested that it is the long-term family disturbance which leads to the antisocial disorder rather than the short period of care. The authors stress that families seeking short-term placement for their children frequently need help long after the crisis leading to placement is over.

YULE, W. and RAYNES, N. (1972) 'Behavioural characteristics of children in residential care in relation to indices of separation', *Journal of Child Psychology and Psychiatry,* 13, 4.

Scope and purpose Examines the adjustment of children living in two local authority children's homes and the experiences related to their care which are associated with emotional/behavioural disturbance.

Sample Seven hundred and seventy-six children in two large group cottage homes run by the Children's Department of a large urban local authority. All the children under the age of 11 years received their education at primary and nursery schools within the grounds of the homes. All but 15 children aged over 11 attended local authority

secondary schools.
Control data on children not in residential care were collected only for those attending secondary schools.

Method Background data were collected from regularly reviewed and updated case records prepared by child care officers.
Measures of adjustment consisted of the behaviour scales developed by Rutter (1967) and used subsequently in the Isle of Wight studies. Houseparents completed a 30 item Scale A for each child and teachers were asked to complete the 26 item Scale B. In all both scales were completed on 584 children (75 per cent of total).
To establish whether the degree of deviance found in this group of children is higher than that in the normal population the data were compared with three other sets of data using the same behaviour scales on children living in their own homes.

Findings 1. Not all children in care were perceived either by houseparents or teachers as 'deviant'.
2. Significantly more children in care were rated as deviant by both houseparents and teachers than were children whose homes are on the Isle of Wight.
3. Significantly more children in care at secondary school age were rated by their teachers as deviant compared with children attending the same schools but living in their own homes.
4. Significantly more children in care than those living with their own families in a working class borough in London were rated by their teachers to be deviant.
5. Looking only at teachers' ratings, examination of the relationship between behavioural adjustment and placement experiences showed that age at first placement had no consistent relationship with teachers ratings of behaviour.
6. There was a slight tendency for the data to support the argument that the greater the proportion of life spent in care the more likely the child will be rated as maladjusted.
7. There was only slight evidence to support the argument that the greater the length of current stay the child experiences, the more maladjusted he is likely to be.
8. The data suggests that children experiencing their first placement in care are likely to be rated as less maladjusted.

Conclusion The data demonstrates that these children in care are more likely to be maladjusted than their peers living in their own homes. The data provide little to support the argument that the age at which a child first leaves home or the number of surrogate homes he has as a result of separation from his own family, are related to later behaviour.

iii) What Kind of Care Works?

ALDERTON, F.R. (1972) 'The residential treatment response of disturbed children, using serial ratings of adjustment', *Journal of Canadian Psychiatry Association,* 17, 4.

Scope and purpose An examination of the treatment response of 20 children from admission to discharge, using ratings by child care staff. The study seeks to investigate the patterns of response and to see whether response to treatment can be predicted and if so how early.

Sample Nineteen boys and one girl. A diagnosis of behaviour disorder, neurotic behaviour disorder or neurotic character disorder had been made in 17 children; three boys were diagnosed as schizophrenic. All were judged capable of responding favourably to the therapeutic milieu.

Method Change following treatment and the effectiveness of treatment was measured by the Children's Pathology Index. Ratings were made at approximately six weekly intervals with an additional observation two to four weeks after admission.

Findings At discharge 12 children were classed as 'responders' and eight as 'non-responders'. Those children who did not respond early made no gains during the latter half of hospitalization. A satisfactory outcome was best predicted by the total rating change within the first six months as a percentage of the treatment interval.

CRISS, F. and GOODWIN, R. (1970) 'Short-term group counseling for parents of children in residential treatment', *Child Welfare,* 49, 1.

Describes a 12-week parent group counselling programme initiated by a welfare department in Virginia, USA.

Weekly sessions were held with eight parent-couples and one single parent in an effort to give parents a chance to examine their relationship with their children and themselves and to gain insight into their child's problems as extensions of the total family relationship.

The 23 weeks concluded with generally supportive comments from the therapists and positive reactions from the group. The therapists considered that several weeks later there were signs of significant effort towards change in several of the families.

The implication is that public welfare has a responsibility to move further into the treatment of parents while their children are in residential treatment, group homes or foster care.

DAVIS, L.F. (1971) 'Recommendation, placement and provision: reception centre survey', *Social Work Today*, 1, 10.

Over a four year period the records of case conferences held on 200 children at a reception centre were kept with a view to obtaining 1) Some indication of the value of conference recommendations in their present form, 2) Information regarding the placement of children with specific and for related problems (e.g. non-attendance at school and stealing), 3) An appraisal of the resources available as a guide for future needs.

The basic data is summarized in table form giving the family situation at the time of the child's admission, age group, IQ, and the recommendation made at the case conference. Extracts from case review reports provide further illustration and there is also a general assessment of the children's present situation.

It is concluded that for varied groups of children there is an acknowledged lack of provision, while for others there is a need to examine more closely treatment methods in relation to individual problems. Overall, there is a need to develop selection techniques so that better use can be made of available resources.

ENDRES, V.J. and GOKE, D.H. (1973) 'Time-out rooms in residential treatment centres', *Child Welfare*, 52, 6.

This article refers to the use of time-out rooms, frequently referred to as control rooms, seclusions and quiet rooms, as a treatment technique in residential treatment centres.

A 16 item questionnaire was sent to 50 residential centres treating emotionally disturbed children in Iowa, Minnesota and Wisconsin. Forty-two replies were received and from these it was found that 40 per cent of residential homes had a control room. The reported findings include the use made of such a room and the attitudes of staff and children towards it.

There was considerable variation in replies to the questionnaire. If a general philosophy exists, it seems to be that a time-out room should be used as a treatment to help the child regain or establish inner controls and ego integration, that enable the child to recognize limits, reduce regressive tendencies, and enhance coping ability.

FLINT, B.M. (1967) *The Child and the Institution; a Study of Deprivation and Recovery,* University of London Press.

Scope and purpose This study records observations made of a group of infants and young children in a children's home administered by the Catholic Children's Aid Society of Toronto. Over a four year period 85 children were studied before, during and after a period of treatment, in order to assess the degree to which early deprivation can be relieved. Following some early findings, the children's home was reorganized and a new treatment programme initiated. The setting up of this programme and the progress achieved form the major part of this project.

First Project

Sample The initial project involved nine children aged between 22 months and three years. These children were regarded as an experimental group permitting evaluation of how much a play programme could contribute to their recovery.

Method A play programme was designed and toys and play equipment were obtained for a playroom resembling that of a normal nursery school, but adapted to the children's immaturity. The playroom was open for two hours each day for approximately four and a half months, and was supervised by two trained staff. At first the children were brought to the playroom one at a time by the supervisor. Each child was treated differently, according to the supervisor's evaluation of his emotional state and his probable response. Daily records were kept by the supervisors of the children's responses to this programme.

Results After four and a half months only five children could play together constructively for a short time and at no time did a group pattern evolve resembling those found in nursery school playrooms. Varying degrees of improvement however could be noted in the play habits of most of the children. Six of the nine children became capable of following their individual play interest for a short while, even with a few other children in the room. It was judged that these six showed slight signs of improved mental health. The children's speech which had been grossly defective at the beginning of the experiment showed substantial improvement.

None of the nine children seemed to have any capacity or readiness for social activity.

Implications The limited response both to adults and to the play situation indicated that qualities essential for mental health were lacking. To effect any real improvement in mental health would involve a complete change of programme, a new staff willing to gear the programme to the needs and abilities of the children and a greatly increased staff to provide the necessary direction, care, love and control. A total reorganization of the home was recommended.

Main Project

In the light of these findings and recommendations the children's home was reorganized and sweeping environmental changes were made. The actual building was remodelled and the number of staff doubled to provide one staff member for every child. A variety of methods of staff training were employed and assessed. In addition a large group of volunteer 'mothers' were trained, one of whom was assigned to each child. Playrooms and playgrounds were adapted to meet each child's developmental level.

The main project sample consisted of 85 children. The children's reactions to the new programme were recorded on the Infant Security Scale previously developed at the Institute of Child Study, Toronto University. According to this scale a variety of symptoms of behaviour significant to mental health are listed in terms of the theory of 'security', which is based on the belief that trust in others and trust in oneself and one's world form the core of mental health.

Findings Constant reassessment of the children on the Infant Security Scales revealed a marked improvement in many of the children after the first year of treatment. After 18 months many showed signs of mental health sufficient to be considered ready for placement in homes. A social worker was employed to help choose particular homes to meet their specific needs.

The case histories of five children describe their progress in detail. They were selected to represent different personalities and different responses to therapy.

The final section of this report details the operating costs of the children's home throughout the study period.

Conclusions The treatment programme demonstrated the degree to which children with greatly differing personalities can respond to an enriched and benign environment and revealed the intensity of their needs for adults who care for them.

It was concluded that four important principles must be maintained if an institution is to promote healthy development — individuality, dependent relationships, opportunities for initiative in the children, and consistency of care and discipline.

GEISER, R.L. (1971) 'An experimental program of activity therapy in a child care center', *Child Welfare*, 50, 5.

The author describes two years experience of using psychodramatic techniques in dealing with living problems in a residential child care centre.

Sixteen girls aged seven to nine years were divided into two groups each led by two adults. They met at regular intervals to put on plays which they made up about life in their cottage. Using such techniques as sociodrama, psychodrama and sensitivity exercises the staff involved tried to 'intervene in crises, build egos, aid adjustment, give information, develop empathy for others and improve impulse control'. The technique was later tried with children from five to 14 years and found suitable for all ages and was considered to be very successful, although the criteria used to judge success are not specified in this article.

GREENBERG, A. and MAYER, M.F. (1972) 'Group home care as an adjunct to residential treatment', *Child Welfare*, 51, 7.

A study of 59 children who were discharged from a residential treatment centre for emotionally disturbed children to group homes containing four or five children and one or two foster parents. The group home experience is described as a transitional one bridging the gap between the time of a child's readiness to leave the treatment centre and the time of his readiness to return to his family or live independently.

Factors relating to the readiness of the child to end his treatment in residential care and to his need for continued treatment are discussed. The children's progress in group homes is compared with their adjustment at the residential treatment centre.

Of the 59 children in the sample, 18 did not adjust well in the group home.

For the 41 who were considered to have adjusted successfully, the group home was seen to fulfill one or more of the following needs:
1. It provided accommodation when their own home was not available.
2. It provided accommodation when their own home was temporarily unavailable to them.
3. It provided an opportunity to live in the community and receive further treatment services.
4. It provided a transitional protective environment in which to gain support and strength.

5. It enabled a renewal of acquaintance with their parents on a more realistic basis than the institutional climate permitted.

6. It represented a further motivation for both parents and children.

HEITING, K. (1971) 'Involving parents in residential treatment of children', *Children*, 18, 5.

This article describes the work of a treatment centre for emotionally disturbed boys that has been experimenting with ways in which to involve parents in the treatment of the children in its care.

On referral the child and his parents participate in a pre-placement conference and throughout the child's stay, parents are encouraged to participate in the treatment programme. They are required to attend regular casework therapy sessions with a social worker and parent discussion groups are held monthly. They are also included in the periodic evaluation of their child's progress and have the chance to attend parent/teacher conferences where they can discuss the child's school work and his adjustment to the classroom.

Results of this parent involvement programme cannot be adequately assessed but over a four year period there has been a gradual decrease in the average length of stay at the centre, from 36 months for those boys discharged in 1968 to 30.5 months for those discharged in the earlier part of 1971.

JOHNSON, R. (1967) 'Foster grandparents in America', *Child Care News*, No 65.

This article describes the Foster Grandparents Project, a demonstration project sponsored by the American government and designed to give employment to needy persons over the age of 60. (Also 'Foster grandparents for emotionally disturbed children', *Children*, 14, 2, 1967).

MAN KEUNG HO (1971) 'Problems and results of a shift to heterogeneous age groups in cottages at a boys home', *Child Welfare*, 50, 9.

This article documents the process in a boys home of changing from cottage groups set up according to age similarity to groups with a wide range of ages.

It is concluded that the experience produced far more positive than negative results. Positive changes on the part of the boys were attributed in part to improved staff morale and a greater willingness to innovate.

MORA, G. *et al.* (1969) 'A residential treatment center moved towards the community mental health model', *Child Welfare*, 48, 10.

This paper reports on ten years experience of a pilot project in residential treatment of emotionally disturbed children and describes how a treatment centre, originally conceived of as a social environment isolated from the community has gradually moved towards the community in an attempt to integrate the therapeutic approach with the positive aspects of community life.

The Astor Home for Children was established in 1953 as a pilot project of the New York State Mental Health Commission, to determine the effectiveness of residential treatment of emotionally disturbed children who could no longer be maintained in home, school, or community, but who were not so severely impaired as to warrant hospitalization.

Although the original programme was concerned exclusively with treatment and rehabilitation of children so seriously disturbed that separation from their family was necessary, work is now being done with children who remain in and are treated with their families. The Home has also joined with the local schools in a study of environmental factors that affect children's personality development.

PATTON, J.L. (1969) 'Social impacts of moving a residential treatment centre from city to country setting', *Child Welfare*, 48, 8.

A report of the effects on both children and staff when a residential centre for 56 boys and girls was moved from a city residential neighbourhood to newly built facilities in a country setting. The findings are impressionistic rather than quantitative.

Despite early problems, the increased space, new facilities and a rural setting raised school productivity, stablized adolescents' job experiences and cut down on vandalism. The staff situation became more stable and parents became more receptive to their children's placement.

PIZZAT, F. (1973) *Behaviour Modification in Residential Treatment for Children: Model of a Program*, New York, Behavioural Publications.

This book, written essentially for people who work in residential treatment centres for children, is about the identification and utilization of some appropriate psychological principles.

Based on his experience in working with emotionally disturbed children the author first defines the basic principles of the operant conditioning model of treatment, and then describes the implementation of this programme at a residential centre for children with emotional and/or behavioural problems.

Central to this approach to treatment is the adoption of a system of 'artificial reinforcement', which dispenses 'rewards' and 'punishments' for 'appropriate' and 'misappropriate' behaviour. The programme is based on a central thesis that behaviour is influenced by its consequences and that what follows behaviour influences its recurrence — i.e. in order to change behaviour it is necessary to pay attention to the consequences of that behaviour.

POLSKY, H.W. and CLASTER, D.S. (1968) *The Dynamics of Residential Treatment: Social System Analysis,* University of North Carolina Press.

This research was part of a series of investigations conducted at the Hawthorn Cedar Knolls School — a treatment centre for emotionally disturbed and delinquent boys and girls. The present study was set up 'to observe differences in cottage-care orientation and management modes and their consequences for the peer-group organization.' It examines and compares three residential cottages for senior boys looking at specific situations, interactions and behaviour patterns within a theoretical framework — namely, the social system theory of Parsons and Bales.

The data is based on the observations made, over a four-week period, by research workers who had been introduced into the cottages. Methods of staff functioning in each of the three cottages, individual counsellor's methods and differences among cottage peer groups are assessed.

The four functions of child care in the cottages-monitoring, guidance, support and integration — are illustrated with examples from the research observers' recordings.

RAWSON, H.E. (1973) 'Residential short-term camping for children with behaviour problems: a behaviour-modification approach', *Child Welfare,* 52, 8.

Describes a short-term therapeutic programme run in two intensive 10 day sessions; the first for boys ages 8-11; the second for boys aged 11-14, and discusses the goals and outcomes of an intensive treatment camping programme for children with behaviour problems.

Tests were given on the second and last day of the camping sessions to ascertain any attitudinal or behavioural changes due to the camp programme itself.

Conclusions Short-term therapeutic camping sessions can be effective in helping social work agencies deal with specific problematic behaviour in children.

Significant gains in academic attitudes and skills can be accomplished with behavioural gain if the material is programmed on the assumption that poor school performance often compounds other problems the child may face.

Follow-up work is essential to maintain and enlarge behavioural gains made. Children enjoy camp life and activities, thereby enabling therapy to be conducted in an atmosphere where their motivation toward participation is at a high level.

WOLINS, M. (1969) *Child Care in Cross-Cultural Perspective; Final Report*, Berkeley, California, University of California. *Mimeograph.*

Scope and purpose The final report — in summary form — of a study designed to evaluate the group care of children in several Eastern European countries and in Israel.

Samples The study comprises ten categories of children in four countries — Austria, Israel, Poland and Yugoslavia.

1. Israel — Kibbutz Youth Group. Approximately 300 children mainly of low socioeconomic status from major Israeli cities and development towns who entered group care in the Kibbutz at approximately 13 years of age and remained there from three to five years.

2. Israel — Youth Village Children. Approximately 100 children, aged from 13 to 17, mainly recent immigrants, who were temporarily sent into group care.

3. Israel — Kibbutz-Born Children. Thirty-three children born and reared in several adjacent Kibbutzim and attending a regional Kibbutz school. The children were aged from 15 to 17 years.

4. Israel — Children Living at Home. Approximately 100 children of recent immigrants settled in development towns.

5. Austria — SOS Kinderdorf. Sixty-five children aged 12 to 18 years, mostly dependent, neglected or abandoned wards of the welfare department. Few maintained substantial ties with their natural family and many were illegitimate.

6. Austria — Children Living at Home. Sixty-two children, aged 12 to 15 years from families living in same community where the Kinderdorf studied was located.

7. Poland — Children's Institution. Thirty-four abandoned and/or

neglected children from Warsaw who were sent to the institution by the local educational and judicial authorities. These children, aged from 11 to 19 years were expected to remain in the institution for all or most of their childhood.

8. Poland — Children Living at Home. A comparison group of 49 children who lived in the neighbourhood of the institution and attended the same schools as the institution children.

9. Yugoslavia — Children's Institution. Approximately 100 children living in four institutions near Belgrave. The majority were sent to the institution by local social work centres. Ages ranged from 11 to 19 years.

10. Yugoslavia — Children Living at Home. A comparison sample of 76 children living with their parents in the same area as the institutions.

Method A number of tests and observations were made:

Intellectual problem-solving capability was evaluated in terms of performance on the Raven Progressive Matrices Test.

Psychosocial development was evaluated on the basis of the Murray Thematic Apperception Test (TAT).

Several Questionnaires, a sentence completion test and, in some settings, a sociometric test were designed to test certain value areas.

Findings 1. Loss of intellectual capability that may be attributed to separation and placement did not seem to be evident in any of the five group care settings.

2. Children placed before the age of six and tested in adolescence tended to have the same RPM scores and value characteristics as children of the same age who were placed considerably later.

3. The ability to transmit values appears related to the clarity and consistency with which they are held by adults in the child's environment. In this respect the kinderdorf and kibbutz appeared to be the more able to transmit these values.

Conclusion Given that the positive outcomes of certain forms of group care are accepted as fact, the author considers the possibility of achieving them in the United States. The major requirements of 'success' in a residential setting are seen to be:

1. 'An assumption of undeveloped capability rather than of sickness when conceptualizing the condition of the dependent, neglected, deprived or disturbed child.

2. An ideologically clear and strong environment.

3. A setting with strong peer influences and the capability to offer not only help, guidance and challenges, but also the models and opportunities of adult membership.

iv) **Residential Staff**

CENTRAL COUNCIL FOR EDUCATION AND TRAINING IN SOCIAL WORK (1974) *Social Work: Residential Work is a part of Social Work. Report of the Working Party on Education for Residential Social Work.* Central Council for Education and Training in Social Work (Paper 3).

The report of the Working Party on education for residential social work. The Working Party was set up to:

1. Review the existing pattern of training for residential work.
2. Consider the levels of training needed.
3. Develop proposals for a scheme of training in residential social work.

Method The following six patterns of training for residential work were considered and rejected.

1. The present system.
2. A separate pattern of training for residential work.
3. The social work/welfare work model.
4. CQSW by full-time study only.
5. A two-part CQSW.
6. A phased scheme leading to the CQSW.

An initial discussion document was circulated to statutory and voluntary agenices, government departments, and other relevant bodies. About 500 items of feedback were received; these were analysed and are partly summarized in the appendices to the report.

Recommendations In all 46 recommendations were made; they include:

1. The majority of the Working Party favour a two tier pattern of training. The first tier of training would lead to a certificate which would be a recognized national qualification. The suggested title is 'Certificate of Proficiency in Social Work'. The second tier qualification should be the CQSW.
2. The Council should begin discussions with the Open University to explore the possibility of jointly creating a modular scheme for the CQSW.
3. There should be a single pattern of training for field and residential social workers.
4. The Council should promote new courses which specialize in the teaching of methods of intervention related to work with groups and

communities.

5. Management studies should be an effective area in basic social work courses and there should be opportunities for advanced study and research in this subject.

6. The Senior Certificate in the Residential Care of Children and Young People should be considered as at least the equivalent of the CQSW.

7. The same salary scales should apply for all social workers but residential workers should be appointed at points substantially higher on the scales because of the added responsibilities and inconveniences of their work.

8. Student visits should be set up in certain residential centres to meet the need for suitable practical work placements.

THE CHILD IN CARE (1968a) 'The New Institution: Some consideration of New Buildings for Children and Young People in Care. Part I: A Children's Home within a High Density Housing Development', *Child in Care*, 8, 12.

The first in a series of articles considering new buildings for children and young people in care.

Each article contains some account of the area and department it serves with the demographic, economic, social and geographic characteristics of the environment. The need for a new building is also shown and the architect then describes his brief and gives some account of his approach to the problem, including drawings, plans etc.

The first article describes a children's home within a high density housing development.

DR BARNARDO'S (1968) *Report of the Working Party on the Conditions of Work of Residential Staff in Dr Barnardo's*, Hertford, Dr Barnardo's.

Scope and purpose Report of a Working Party set up to consider conditions of service for residential staff.

Method Questionnaires were completed by superintendents and heads of schools on behalf of their staff. Information was obtained on such items as staff accommodation and amenities, hours of work and time off. Further comments were obtained on problems concerning married staff and their children, the employment of male staff and staff participation in the running of the homes. In all 93 questionnaires were completed from various types of residential establishments.

Findings Forty-seven recommendations are discussed under three main headings: 1. Long hours of work. 2. Staff amenities and lack of privacy for staff and their families. 3. Staff development.

JAFFE, E.D. (1970) 'The impact of experimental services on dependent children referred for institutional care', *Social Work Today*, 1, 2.

A study concerning services to dependent children and their parents, in Israel.

Two local public welfare offices in Israel were operated for a period of 18 months by a university guided team of social workers to test the effects of innovative work on the rate of institutional placements for children referred to the agencies. A comparison of placement outcomes was made between cases from the two experimental offices and two control offices where services proceeded as usual. The major difference between the experimental offices and the two control offices was the assignment in the experimental settings of all referrals for institution placement to research social workers using a more imaginative approach to case management than was common in other welfare office settings. In both experimental and control offices case management was recorded in detail by the workers on a monthly basis.

Findings At the close of the study there was a significant drop in institutional placements in the experimental offices and a striking increase in foster home and own-home placements. Of the children placed in institutions 61 per cent were from the control group compared with 39 per cent from the experimental offices.

The study showed that the experimental offices concentrated first on personal counselling, income maintenance and home care services while the control offices concentrated much less on personal counselling, slightly more on providing material needs and very heavily on planning institutional placement.

KRAUSE, K. (1974) 'Authoritarianism, dogmatism and coercion in child caring institutions: a study of staff atttitudes', *Child Welfare*, 53, 1.

The purpose of this study was to identify particular factors associated with staff attitudes on dimensions of authoritarianism, dogmatism, and coercion. Specifically it examines the association between staff attitudes and the type of institution in which they were employed and the position held in the institution.

Method The sample consisted of 19 child caring institutions with 'vastly different kinds of programmes' — in the Chicago area. All the staff in these institutions were included in the study and asked to complete a written questionnaire. Of the 344 questionnaires distributed 286 were returned (84 per cent). The institutions were classified into three types, as Intensive Treatment, Treatment, or Group Care. The criteria determining classification were — provision and frequency of individual treatment, use and amount of psychiatric consultation, institution size, staff-child ratio, staff supervision, professional training of staff, and size of living unit.

The questionnaire was designed in three parts to cover 1) Demographic characteristics of the respondents, 2) A problem solving exercise dealing with different types of incidents involving children in institutional settings (C Scale), 3) The D (Dogmatism) Scale and the F (Authoritarianism) Scale.

Analysis of variance tests were used to examine the relationship between scores on the C, D and F scales and the primary variables. Correlations were used to examine the relationships between the three scales.

Findings It was found that Intensive Treatment programmes provided climates that were most open, conducive to forming close relationships, flexible and most normative in handling child behaviour problems, while Group Care programmes were most closed, structured, formed in relationships and coercive in handling child behaviour problems.

Caseworkers were found to be least authoritarian and most open-minded in their attitudes and favoured the least coercive methods. Supervisors and administrators were equally open-minded but were more authoritarian and favoured more coercive methods. Residential Child Care workers were most authoritarian, least open-minded and favoured the most coercive control methods.

The author concludes that the attitudes of staff members in child caring institutions are related to their position in the institution and to the types of institution in which they are employed. The findings suggest that there are ways in which attitudinal climates can be influenced through selection, training and interaction of personnel, but these are not outlined.

LUTHERAN COUNCIL IN THE USA (1972) 'A perspective on residential child care programs', *Child Welfare*, 51, 1.

This article presents the conclusions of a survey of Lutheran residential child care programmes published in December 1970. Twenty-nine institutions were studied.

Institution administrators identified the following as the major changes of the last decade:

1. An upgrading of the position of child care workers.
2. Improved physical facilities to provide for more individualized care and treatment of children.
3. A reduction in the length of stay of children.
4. A decrease in the size of the child population and, at the same time an increase in staff.
5. A change in the characteristics of the child being referred for placement (older, more disturbed and from more disintegrated families).
6. An increased emphasis on the treatment orientation.

As problems confronting the institutions the administrators cited:

1. Lack of qualified, trained child care workers.
2. Lack of adequate resources within the child's home community when he is ready for discharge.
3. The need for more intensive work with the families of children accepted for care.

MORE, W.S. (1973) 'The personality of residential staff', *Residential Social Work*, 13, 2.

In an effort to identify some kind of personality profile of the residential child care officer, a small pilot study was completed with the cooperation of students on a residential child care course and students on a social work course.

Both groups were found to be no more extrovert or introvert than the normal population. Social Work students were found to be fairly normally stable emotionally but residential students revealed a very strong and consistent shift from the normal in an unstable direction. They also provided much evidence of great feelings of anxiety, inferiority and guilt coupled with a strong need for support, approval and acceptance.

NEY, E. and TOMLINSON, D.F. (1972) 'Children in long-term care: a new approach', *Social Work Today*, 3, 2.

This article describes the formation and progress of a specialist section of Tower Hamlets Social Services Department dealing specifically with children in in long-term care.

The existence of a long-stay section is seen to be of value firstly because it can be successfully isolated from the ever increasing tide of work flowing the way of area terms, secondly because more thorough work can lead to better relationships between the department and client and a reduction in crisis and crisis action, and thirdly because control over intake can leave room for experiment.

A group work project with 15 mainly pre-adolescent children selected from children's homes and foster homes is described as the section's most interesting innovation.

RESIDENTIAL CHILD CARE ASSOCIATION (1968a) 'The memorandum: findings of a working party set up to consider the Administration of Children's Homes Regulations 1951 and the Memorandum by the Home Office on the Conduct of Children's Homes', *Child in Care*, 8, 3.

Report of the Working Party set up by the Residential Child Care Association to investigate and make specific recommendations on the current relevance of the Regulations and Memorandum.

SCOTTISH CHILDREN'S OFFICERS' ASSOCIATION (1967) *Memorandum on Staffing and Conditions in Local Authority Children's Homes*, Edinburgh, Scottish Children's Officers' Association.

Reports the findings and recommendations of an *ad hoc* committee set up 'to inquire into the administration, staffing, salaries and conditions of service of Local Authority Children's Homes in Scotland'.

Summary of the main recommendations

1. Staff-child ratios should be one staff to every three children under five years and one staff to every eight children over five years.

2. A normal basic working week should be taken to be one of 42 hours.

3. A responsibility allowance should be paid in respect of hours worked over and above the 42 hours where a family pattern is in operation.

4. Minimum off-duty time should be prescribed. It is suggested that this should be three hours daily, one-and-a-half days weekly and one weekend of three days every four weeks.

5. Some award, such as the declaration of experience should be granted to well experienced, older members of staff and this should

entitle the holder to the same award that goes with the Certificate in Residential Child Care.

6. Housemothers in charge of homes of 10-15 places should be paid the same salary as a deputy matron in a home of 15-25 places.

7. A 'homes committee with membership drawn from both the Children's Officers' Association and the Residential Child-Care Association should be set up on a permanent basis.

Included as an appendix is a postscript following the publication of the Williams Report — *Caring for People*, (see *Residential Child Care: Facts and Fallacies*, Page 209) which sets out the findings and recommendations of the Report relevant to some of the specific issues discussed in this Memorandum. It illustrates the broad similarity of many of the recommendations.

SCOTTISH COUNCIL OF SOCIAL SERVICE: COMMITTEE ON CO-OPERATION IN CHILD CARE (1967) *An Enquiry into the Needs and Resources of Residential Child Care Institutions in Scotland*, Paisley, South Council of Social Service.

A survey of local authority and voluntary children's homes in Scotland designed to investigate whether any large amount of accommodation was not being used and to pinpoint those areas of residential child care under heavy and constant pressure.

In all 86 voluntary homes and 96 local authority homes were surveyed and the information obtained was concerned with children in four main categories — normal children, physically handicapped children, mentally handicapped children or maladjusted children.

Conclusion No significant amount of unused residential accommodation was found. Concern was expressed that there was no general margin of unused accommodation which might meet increased demands in the future.

The pressure on children's homes catering for mentally handicapped and maladjusted children was such that there was a real need for further places.

Present training facilities, recruitment and conditions of residential service were unsatisfactory — this was borne out in figures produced by certain local authorities who reported that, due to continuous under-staffing, homes had been unable to take the number of children for which they were originally designed.

TUTT, N. (1972) 'A study of attitudes expressed by field and residential social workers', *Social Service News*, 2, 6.

Scope and purpose A study designed to evaluate how much the division between field workers and residential social workers can be attributed to 'differences in personality' and to examine how field and residential workers compare to other social workers, namely psychiatric nurses and to the general population.

Sample and method The Wilson Scale of Conservatism was used to test the attitudes of a sample of 38 field workers and 37 residential workers undergoing full-time training. All had previously been employed in social work and there were no significant differences in the educational background of the two groups.

Analysis of variance was carried out to test the effects of age and sex as well as job.

Findings Social workers are not a homogeneous group and are likely to express different attitudes depending on where they work, their age and their sex.

Female social workers whether field or residential scored higher on conservatism than male social workers.

Social workers over 30 years of age were significantly more conservative than those under 30 years.

Residential social workers were significantly more conservative than fieldworkers.

Social workers as a group were seen to be slightly less conservative than psychiatric nurses and more liberal than the general population.

WILTSHIRE COUNTY COUNCIL CHILDREN'S COMMITTEE (1967) 'Residential child care provision. Report of the Working Party on residential child care provision in Wiltshire', *Child in Care*, 7, 5.

The findings of a Working Party set up to consider the amount and suitability of accommodation for children, the gaps in provision and staffing and related matters. The report was compiled for use in formulating a five-year development programme. It is in two parts. The first deals with accommodation requirements for children; appendices at the end of the report give some relevant figures and also a list of residential establishments. The second part is concerned mainly with staff matters, such as accommodation, roles, job satisfaction and staff development.

PART II
Other Literature

---

i) Policy and Practice

ADLER, J. (1971) 'Interpersonal relationships in residential treatment centres for disturbed children', *Child Welfare,* 50, 4.

This article discusses three types of interpersonal relationships within a residential treatment centre for emotionally disturbed children. They include relationships between children and staff, among children within their peer groups and among residential staff. The therapeutic effectiveness of a residential treatment centre is held to be largely dependent on the relationships within and among the groups involved.

AINSWORTH, F. and BRIDGFORD, N. (1972) 'Necessary trends in residential care', *British Hospital Journal,* 22nd July.

An article concerned with the evaluation of residential care and treatment programmes. It is suggested that new residential units may be outdated at the moment of inception if there is no adequate planning of programmes of care, and realistic supervision of staff and evaluation.

AKHURST, B.A. (1972) 'The effects of long stay care', *Concern,* 9.

A short review of some current studies raising issues relevant to all forms of residential care. In particular, three areas of research are discused — language development; personal relationships; and social development.

ASSOCIATION OF SOCIAL WORKERS (1967) *'New Thinking about Institutional Care'.* Papers from a conference organized by the Association of Social Workers.

This is a collection of some of the papers given at a conference organized by the Education Subcommittee of the Association of Social Workers in 1967. The aim of the conference was to provide an opportunity for caseworkers, residential staff, and social work administrators to consider the different types of institutional care. The first paper discusses the development of institutional care in Britain from the early nineteenth century, while the second examines the structure and dynamics of institutions. The following papers are concerned with different types of residential care; they include an outline of the development of residential child care and a discussion of the relationship between residential staff and the child care officer. The remaining papers deal specifically with adults in institutions.

BALBERNIE, R. (1972) *Residential Work with Children,* 2nd Edition, Chaucer Publishing Company, for Human Context Books.

A discussion of residential care for maladjusted children. It gives an account of the past development of residential care of maladjusted and delinquent children, examines the present provision in this field and suggests how more effective and relevant help can be given to such children in the future.

The work reported is based on the author's experience of child guidance clinics and residential special schools and includes many illustrative case histories.

BARKER, P. (1973) *Care can Prevent; Child Care or Child Psychiatry?* National Children's Home.

A convocation lecture of the National Children's Home. This essay looks at ways in which the prevalence of psychiatric disorders in children might be reduced. It examines first, the size of the problem as documented in recent research studies and goes on to describe a particular group of disturbed children in care. Causative factors and methods of prevention are discussed in general with reference to specific research projects.

BEEDELL, C.J. (1970) *Residential Life with Children,* Routledge and Kegan Paul.

An introductory text which gives a general assessment of the provisions, resources and problems involved in residential work.

The first chapter discusses the scope of residential work with children and describes an imaginary 'ideal type' residential unit. Three chapters examine the children's needs and both the theory and practice of meeting them. The residential worker's task is then discussed together with some implications of this for staffing and structure, and some of the inherent problems.

An appendix outlines the range and variety of residential provision for children and young people.

BEEDELL, C.J. (1967) 'Residential work in Denmark', *Child Care*, 21, 2.

A report of the author's study tour of residential institutions in Denmark with comparisons between the scope and pattern of responsibility of residential work in Denmark and in Britain.

The bulk of residential provision in Denmark is carried by private institutions which are very largely state-subsidized and a central directorate of the child care service is responsible for the placing of children.

As regards the type of treatment being offered the author was impressed by a strong emphasis on parental responsibility and on continuing contact with the parents. The good physical conditions of the institutions visited are mentioned and also their close links with the surrounding community. There is considerable emphasis on educational stimulus, with generous and imaginative provision for play opportunities and always some kind of workshop facility. The children are given and are expected to take a fair share of responsibility for themselves. This shared responsibility and educationally stimulating provision is well backed by professional psychologists and social workers, often employed by the institution.

BERRY, J. (1972) 'The experience of reception into residential care', *British Journal of Social Work*, 2, 4.

This article considers the experience of first entering residential care from the viewpoint of the newcomers and from the view points of the established inmates and the staff who receive him.

After dealing with the initial human interactions and reactions at the point of admission the author goes on to discuss ways of easing the impact of reception.

BLOOM, C.V. (1969) *Children are our Concern; the Story of One*

Voluntary Society (Dr Barnardo's) in the Post-War Period. Dr Barnado's.

This book, written by a former chief medical officer of Dr Barnardo's, describes in detail the child care operations of Dr Barnardo's.

It begins with a brief account of the developing child care service in the post-war period, with some of the implications for Barnardo's of the relevant government legislation. The following chapters describe in more detail the important aspects of Barnardo's work. These include admission, both under voluntary agreements and on payment by local authorities; adoption; fostering; the various types of residential group care; and staff training. Also included are sections dealing with special problems, for example, colour and difficult children – and with special education for the physically handicapped, educationally subnormal and mentally subnormal.

BRAMPTON, W.E. (1967) *Criteria in Placement and the Needs of the Child; a Year of Research and Study 1966/67. Duplicated.*

A view of residential child care by a former residential child care worker. It examines the authority that is vested in a local authority which receives a child into care, and the hierarchical structure of the children's department.

The organization and staffing of reception centres, larger types of children's homes, and family group homes are discussed in relation to the needs of the children, the type of building and the needs of the staff.

BRANDWINE, A. (1969) 'Upbringing of children in kibbutzim of Israel', *Young Children,* 24, 5.

This article describes the origins and basic features of kibbutz culture and then deals with the upbringing of children in one particular kibbutz. The structure of education at different age levels is outlined as the children progress from the infants' house to the toddlers' house to the kindergarten.

BURMEISTER, E. (1967) *Tough Times and Tender Moments in Child Care Work,* New York, Columbia University Press.

This book deals with various aspects of the daily routine in residential child care, using extensive comments by houseparents themselves. The field covered includes creative activities, visiting days, relationships with child care workers and the natural parent and so on.

CALDECOTT COMMUNITY (1971) *Community Living for Children; Two papers presented to the Caldecott Conference in October 1970*, Ashford, Caldecott Community.

1) Community Living for Children — Future needs of child care by M.L. Kellmer Pringle.

This paper discusses the changing professional concepts and aims of residential care, the policy implications of new knowledge arising from studies of child development, some ideas relating specifically to group living for children and finally, the case for comprehensive assessment of children's needs.

2) Planning Services for Children by Joan D. Cooper.

This paper discusses the relationship between the Caldecott Community and the children in its care and considers the implications of the formal machinery of planning set up under the Children and Young Persons Act 1969.

THE CHILD IN CARE (1968b) 'The residential task', *Child in Care*, 8, 2-8.

A series of short articles concerning the varied aspects of residential child care.

The first article — 'The role of the residential services adviser in the support of houseparents' by Jim Hodder suggests that, in the supporting aspect of the job there are three main elements: 1) discussion, guidance and active help, 2) teaching and the development of ideas, 3) the development of staff in relation to the job. Each of these elements is discussed in detail.

The second article is written by a headmistress of a school for deaf children and deals with 'Caring staff in a boarding special school.'

Articles three and four written by Elizabeth Ward deal with 'The work of the residential nursery'. The task of the residential nursery is discussed in two parts: 1) to provide short-term care for 'long-term children' i.e., children for whom there is little hope of immediate fostering or adoption, and 2) to provide specialized care for children with special needs, e.g. those experiencing a sudden, temporary separation, babies for adoption and long-term fostering, children who come into care for a period of rehabilitative casework, and disturbed and handicapped children.

The fifth article — 'Reception centres' by Sheila Lambden — discusses the work of reception centres including some of the various 'reasons of entry' and some of the problems they present.

Finally — 'One view of defining a children's home' by Derek Potts — describes five criteria for a therapeutic community.

DOCKAR-DRYSDALE, B.E. (1968) *Therapy in Child Care*, Longmans.

A collection of papers dealing with children who are severely maladjusted and emotionally deprived. It is intended specifically for students on residential child care courses.

The papers are nearly all concerned with work carried out at the Mulberry Bush School from 1948 to 1963 and are arranged chronologically. They include such subjects as damage and restitution, the residential treatment of 'frozen' children, communications as a technique in treating disturbed children, regression in a structured environment and the therapeutic value of play.

DOCKAR-DRYSDALE, B.E. (1970a) 'Integration and unintegration in residential treatment', *Therapeutic Education*, Spring.

A discussion of the concept of integration in which the author expresses her belief in the problem of incompatibility with which integrated and unintegrated children are burdened if they are living together. There is a description of the setting up of a small internal unit at the Cotswold Community which was explicitly planned for the provision of primary experience. Primary experience is defined as that process which normally takes place during the first year of life, and in which the baby gradually separates out from the mother or mother substitute and becomes a person in his own right. Emotionally deprived children it is said, are those who have not completed this process and as such have not fully developed a 'self'.

DOCKAR-DRYSDALE, B.E. (1970b) 'Meeting children's emotional needs in residential work', *Child in Care*, 10, 9.

This article discusses the concept of therapy based on needs rather than symptoms. The therapy required depends on the stage of integration reached by each individual, and it is therefore necessary to classify children according to needs, based on this degrees of integration. The author provides a rough chart which suggests assumptions, aims and techniques in regard to (a) integrated and (b) unintegrated people of any age from the standpoint of the therapist. Actual therapy, play and consultation and then discussed in detail.

DOREY, R. (1971) 'Personal relationships of a child in care', *Child in Care*, 11, 10.

This article presents a framework of the relationships affecting a child in care and discusses the variety of demands and opportunities that are placed before such a child.

The child in care is brought into direct contact with three more groups than children not in care — 1) 'fellow in-cares', 2) houseparents, 3) children of houseparents, and although he is still involved in a family unit, compared with the child in a normal family, he has so many other channels open to him that conflicts seem inevitable. It is suggested that each relationship is capable of being understood in terms of intensity, proximity, formality, answerability and crisis, and that these five variables are themselves capable of being interpreted over a continuum from one extreme to another. In presenting this framework the author hopes that possible problems concerning the child can be better understood by those involved with him.

GIBBS, J. (1968) *Patterns of Residential Care for Children*, National Children's Home.

A convocation lecture of the National Children's Home. This essay looks at the principles which lie behind different kinds of residential care. After a brief discussion of general principles, five patterns of residential care are discussed in detail, the ordinary small home first, then others with a definite therapeutic aim.

GOLDSTEIN, J., FREUD, A. and SOLNIT, A.J. (1973) *Beyond the Best Interests of the Child*, Collier Macmillan.

A criticism of the existing laws in the United States governing the placement of children.

The authors — two psychoanalysts and a lawyer — argue that the child's interest should be paramount and that while the present laws protect the child's physical well-being they often subordinate his psychological well-being to, for example, an adult's right to assert a biological tie. Some attempt is made to formulate a revised code.

GORE, E. and PHILLIPS, A. (1971) 'The child in care as seen by a child guidance clinic', *Child Care*, 25, 1.

An account of the authors' experiences in working with child care organizations. Observations are made from a child guidance clinic which had a 6 per cent referral of children in care from both local authority and voluntary organization homes.

It is suggested that the psychiatric needs of every child in care should be considered at three stages of his residence in the home.

1) On admission — in consideration of the child's ability to adjust to new surroundings, including the school.

2) During the time of residence — to detect any personality difficulties which may not necessarily be overt.

3) Prior to discharge — to assess future needs, both emotional and educational.

HALFACREE, J. (1972) 'Preparation for care', *Child in Care*, 12, 1.

This article is concerned with the reception of a child into care and discusses ways in which the child can be helped through this period.

HEALTH and SOCIAL SERVICE JOURNAL (1974) 'Residential child care', *Health and Social Service Journal*, 84, 4384.

This article outlines some basic advantages of the 'cottage homes' style of residential care and states that local authorities, who for the past twenty years have been committed to getting rid of their cottage homes are, in some cases, having second thoughts.

There is, for example, renewed interest in the staffing structure of the typical cottage home where the supply of senior resource personnel can provide close but not obtrusive support to those having the day-to-day care of children.

Cottage homes also allow a certain flexibility about the child care itself. Whole families can, for example, be accommodated — if not in the same cottage then at least on the same campus.

Children in cottage homes can also be cushioned against some of the worst effects of changes of staff by the very fact that they relate to a range of relative proximate adults.

The author suggests that many sites have spare land which could be developed for other and public use and that existing common services for whole establishments could be expanded in use to take children from outside the institution. With imagination in making some adjustments to existing regimes cottage homes could become 'more like real and lively villages and less like the ghostly townships they often are at present'.

HIRSCHBERG, J.C. (1970) 'Termination of residential treatment of children', *Child Welfare*, 49, 8.

This article examines the process of termination of residential treatment from the standpoint of the child's parents.

Discharge from residential care usually occurs when therapy is not completely done and this fact must be accepted and planned for by the treatment staff and the parents together.

HOBBS, M. (1973) 'Long term care, Parts I, II & III', *Residential Social Work*, 13, 4, 5 & 6.

A series of three articles concerned with children in long term residential care.

Part I discusses the needs of such children. It is suggested that there are certain groups of children for whom fostering is not likely to provide a desirable or acceptable solution. Among these are sibling groups, children with severe handicaps, children who by reason of their ethnic group are not likely to be accepted as foster children, and adoption and fostering 'breakdowns' who need a period to recover.

The author considers four specific areas of family function and their relation to the provision made in long-term residential care: These are good physical care; education; socialization; and the transmission of values. In respect of these basic needs the residential task may be seen as a three-fold effort — 'to supply what has been omitted, to remedy what has been harmful and to bring to maturity the good experience already received'.

Part II examines the question of staff involvement with children. This must be realistic and there should be recognition from both sides that however significant the child/staff relationship has been the time will come when even if not brought to an end altogether, it will be very much diminished.

In the final Part of this series the author looks further at what 'involvement' means in practice and how residential staff can 'survive' numerous involvements over a long period.

HOLMAN, R. (1968) 'Immigrants and child care policy', *Case Conference*, 15, 7.

Immigrant children have posed a number of questions for children's departments. This article considers the conclusion of Katrine Fitzherbert in 'West Indian Children in London' (1967) that children's departments should administer a different policy towards immigrants, should adopt a tougher line and should refuse more applications.

The author questions this view and suggests that, where care has been refused, immigrant parents frequently turn to the private market in foster homes and daily care which may be far worse than local authority care. Refusal therefore must not be seen as the same as prevention and before turning down applications the caseworker should be sure that, either the child will stay at home, or that the alternative arrangements will be satisfactory.

This article concludes that a truly preventive policy must involve not only casework but improvements in immigrants' physical conditions and greater provision for the daily care of children.

KELLER, R.C. (1973) 'Issues in the residential treatment of children of military personnel', *Child Welfare*, 52, 1.

This article discusses some special problems which arise in the provision of residential treatment for disturbed children of military families, particularly in respect of involving the parents in the planning of therapy.

A father's fears of the effect upon his military career may be a barrier to participation in an effective treatment plan. Both referring agencies and treatment institutions need to be aware of the way in which military family life styles affect the treatment of the child.

KENISTON, K. (1967) 'College students and children in developmental institutions', *Children*, 14, 1.

This article compares the role of the institution for dependent children with that of the student college and in terms of developmental institutions' discusses the similar issues which arise for both groups.

LAW, G. (1971) 'The paramount need in residential work is for a clarification of aims and goals', *Child in Care*, 11, 9.

A sociological discussion of organizational goals in terms of the goal-model conception and the cooperation system and in the context of residential establishments.

Any consideration of the aims and goals of residential work must take into account the fact that residential establishments are organizations and as such exist to meet the various needs of individuals. In this context it is necessary to examine the concept of organizational goals and the application of this concept to residential work.

LENNHOFF, F.G. (1968) *Learning to Live; a Sketch Book for the Residential Worker with Children,* Shrewsbury, Shotton Hall Publications.

This is a sketchbook for the residential worker with children. It comprises a selection of contributions from residential workers writing about their job, and draws on a wide range of experience. It is intended both as a practical book dealing with everyday matters and as a handbook of therapeutic education.

LENNHOFF, F.G. (1970) *Let's Try and Try Again; Studies of Children's Personality Growth in a Residential Setting,* Shrewsbury, Shotton Hall Publications.

This book is concerned with some of the children who have been looked after at Shotton Hall — a school for the treatment and rehabilitation of disturbed and deprived children.

It provides a longitudinal study of the progress of four boys and a rather less detailed account of several others. The introduction, 'ways out of loneliness', describes the author's approach to the problem and indicates the stages of development through which the children have to go on their way towards a 'reality situation'.

LEPINE, A. (1970) 'Health and the immigrant child in care', *Child in Care,* 10, 1 & 2.

Two articles concerned with the needs of immigrant children in care. The first article begins with a discussion of racial prejudice and goes on to consider the cultural backgrounds of immigrants from India, Pakistan and the West Indies. The social factors examined include the generally unfavourable socioeconomic position of immigrants and their poor housing conditions.

The second article provides a broad outline of the development and physical health of immigrant children and the main medical problems facing the public health services. As regards immigrants, these problems are seen to be tuberculosis, dysentery, parasitism and veneral disease.

LEWIS, L.J. (1971) 'A need to regress', *Child in Care*, 11, 10.

This article offers suggestions for residential staff in the practical implementation of the principles of regression in residential child care establishments.

The author distinguishes between a) 'the child who has experienced some good primary fulfilment but insufficient to adequately prepare him for painful stress, and who can benefit from a period of regression to a self-determined level', and b) 'the child whose primary experiences have proved so inadequate that the child is still emotionally functioning at an infantile paranoid stage'.

It is suggested that a special unit should be set up in every children's department, catering for children whose emotional development is severely retarded and who need skilled help. In the first instance, a pilot scheme should be put into effect — perhaps in a small unit of not more than six children divided into two groups of three — behaviour and experiment with techniques of care could then be studied.

LITTNER, N. (1974) 'The challenge to make fuller use of our knowlegde about children', *Child Welfare*, 53, 5.

This article considers the issues of child advocacy, of children's rights and of prevention against the background of current knowledge about the traumatic effects of separation and placement on children.

Some of the common consequences of separation and placement conflicts are discussed and it is argued that although there is now an impressive accumulation of knowledge about such problems, it is not disseminated or utilized to the full.

LYNCH, B. (1970) 'Notes on sources of referral', *Case Conference*, 6, 9.

The author stresses the need to ensure that referring agencies do not over-concentrate on the powers of the children's department to receive children into care at the expense of the department's aims to keep the child in the community.

MAYER, M.F. (1972) 'The group in residential treatment of adolescents', *Child Welfare*, 51, 8.

A discussion of the concept and role of the group in. the residential treatment of adolescents, with an examination of the ways in which 'group experience' can be made a successful therapeutic instrument.

MAYER, M.F. and BLUM, A. (1971) *Healing Through Living: a Symposium on Residential Treatment*, Springfield, Illinois, Charles C. Thomas.

A collection of papers given at a Symposium to consider the place of residential therapy at the present time.

The first chapter presents a historical review covering 100 years of institutional child care at Bellefaire — the residential treatment centre of Cleveland, Ohio. The remaining papers concentrate on three major areas — group living and milieu treatment; special education; and psychotherapy. Much of the work reported concerns Bellefaire itself and there are a number of case histories by way of illustration.

MEYER, M. (1969) 'Family ties and the institutional child', *Children*, 16, 6.

In an effort to maintain some sort of continuing family relationship for children in care the author advises a list of procedures for placement agencies.

These procedures include, for example, involving the child and parents in planning the separation before it takes place, regular family conferences with the child and parents after placement, keeping groups of brothers and sisters together, and follow-up interviews with the family after the child's return home or placement in a foster home.

PARKER, R.A. (1971) *Planning for Deprived Children*, National Children's Home.

A convocation lecture of the National Children's Home. The author examines the problems involved in planning for children in care — particularly in the light of often obscure and conflicting objectives and discusses practical ways in which these problems may be at least ameliorated.

PUGH, E. (1968) *Social Work in Child Care*, Routledge and Kegan Paul.

An introductory account of the child care service which outlines the work of a local authority children's department from the standpoint of a social worker in that setting. It includes a brief historical background and also covers preventive work, the reception of children into care, work with their families during the period of care, foster care, residential care, adoption and the children's department. In each respect the legal and administrative structure of the work is examined as well as the case work aspect.

REDGRAVE, K. (1969) 'Teamwork during reception into care', *Nursery Journal, 59, 572.*

This article discusses the problem of reducing trauma and anxiety when children have to leave home and go into a strange situation, and suggests ways in which the residential and field work members of the team can contribute by working together.

RESIDENTIAL CHILD CARE ASSOCIATION (1970) *Observing Children in Residence: a Guide for Social Workers in Residential Child Care,* Annual Review of Residential Child Care Association.

A collection of short articles based on the theme of the observation of children in residence and its value as one of the tools used in social diagnosis for care and treatment.

RESIDENTIAL CHILD CARE ASSOCIATION (1967) *Play in Child Care,* Annual Review of Residential Child Care Association.

This review, intended for practitioners, is designed as a guide handbook to the meeting of children's play needs within residential child care settings.

RESIDENTIAL CHILD CARE ASSOCIATION (1972) *Conflict,* Annual Review of Residential Child Care Association.

This review brings together a collection of papers concerned with various aspects of conflict in a number of different settings. Included are papers dealing with conflict in the family, with personal conflict, conflicts of identity in substitute care and conflict between the social worker and his clients.

RESIDENTIAL CHILD CARE ASSOCIATION (1969a) *The Residential Task in Child Care; Report of Study Group,* Residential Child Care Association.

The report of a study group set up to consider 'Some of the essential problems of residential child care'.

The basic problems were seen to fall broadly within the outline of the following categories:

1) The children in residential care, 2) Defining the task, 3) The needs of children in groups, 4) Professional training and recruitment, 5) Professional involvement, 6) Staffing Ratios. Each of these aspects is discussed in detail.

RESIDENTIAL CHILD CARE ASSOCIATION (1969b) 'The coloured child in care, Parts I & II', *Child in Care,* 9, 7 & 8.

The report of a working party set up by the Residential Child Care Association to investigate the difficulties experienced by coloured children in care, and the difficulties experienced by people caring for them.

The first part of the report deals with the background culture and customs of immigrants from Pakistan, India and the West Indies, and examines their family structures.

The second part covers the care of the pre-school child, medical aspects of coloured children's care, education and youth services for other children. A further section gives some viewpoints of houseparents on caring for coloured children.

In all, some twenty recommendations are made for future policy and practice. These include, for example, the provision of better facilities for teaching immigrant children, more supportive prevention and the establishment of advice centres, greater provision for the care of pre-school children and the training of residential staff in the background of immigrant children.

RIGHTON, P. (1971) 'The objectives and methods of residential social work', *Child in Care,* 11, 12.

A discussion of the ends and means involved in residential social work.

For the purposes of illustration one type of establishment is used as a model — a long term assessment and treatment unit of medium size for deprived and for emotionally disturbed adolescents.

TIZARD, J. (1974) 'The upbringing of other people's children: implications of research and for research', *Journal of Child Psychology and Psychiatry*, 15, 3.

This paper examines some aspects of the current situation in residential care and describes some ongoing work concerned with the issues raised.

The author looks first at the numbers of children in residential institutions — approximately 92,000 — and illustrates something of 'the heterogeneity of provision which defies explanation except in historical terms'.

The need is felt to assess both personal handicaps and social needs in order to estimate the size of the problem for which services have to be provided. Several recent studies are quoted to demonstrate the progress that has so far been made in developing indicators of individual handicap and family dysfunction, as well as measures of institutional functioning. More research is required however into factors affecting the functioning of complex organizations and into environmental factors affecting child development.

TOD, R.J.N. (1968a) *Children in Care*, Longmans.

This is the first of two volumes containing articles on residential child care and treatment which have, in most cases, appeared in English and American journals during the previous ten years.

It is intended primarily for students on residential child care courses and for residential staff already in the work.

The first three articles examine the child's links with his own family and the distress and anxiety experienced in being received into care. The next three articles deal with some of the practical problems of residential care and describe some practical ways of helping children settle into a new home. This is followed by an account of the particular difficulties that children present to those caring for them and with the difficulties residential workers may have in caring for other people's children.

Two articles describe some ways in which adults and children adapt to each other in a residential setting. A further two discuss the care of difficult adolescents and the final chapter is concerned with staff relationships.

TOD, R.J.N. (1968b) *Disturbed Children,* Longmans.

This is the second of two volumes of collected articles which have appeared in English or American journals in recent years. This book is concerned with the care and treatment of disturbed children who are unable to respond initially to family type care.

The articles included cover such topics as therapeutic practice in group living, communicating with maladjusted children and the process of symbolization, group therapeutic techniques for residential units and psychiatric consultation.

TURNBULL, M. (1972) 'Sensory environments, games and toys for residential communities', *Community Schools Gazette,* 65, 12.

A review of some modern materials available to help alleviate social, psychological and emotional disorders, as they might affect residential communities. Describes some of the exhibits at the Royal College of Art Galleries exhibition entitled 'Playthings for the Handicapped Child'.

VINCENT, B. (1968) *Begone Dull Care; an Informal Guide to the Residential Care of Children,* HMSO.

An informal guide intended to provide a picture of daily life in a children's home and offering practical points for the successful running of the home. It is written specifically for residential child care staff and those considering the profession, and is addressed to housemothers.

WEBER, G.H. and HABERLEIN, B.J. (1972) *Residential Treatment of Emotionally Disturbed Children,* New York, Behavioural Publications.

This selection of readings presents a series of articles — mostly written before 1967 — on the practice of helping emotionally disturbed children in residential settings.

The material is presented in four sections, each section having its own overview:

Section I — Concepts and Strategies — is concerned with the organization, activities and problems of treatment centres.

Section II — Some Treatment Issues — illustrates some of the technical problems of treating children in residential centres. These include, for example, the development of therapeutic relationships with the children, the treatment of children's conflicts, the effects of child/parent separation and the termination of treatment.

Section III — Treatment Approaches — considers the several treatment approaches found in residential centres — education, casework, psychotherapy, group care etc., and shows that individual centres are likely to emphasize different activities and in so doing their programmes may reflect a distinct type.

Section IV — Training and Manpower — contains two articles which focus on staff development, one article which reflects the effects of staff conflict on children and another which illustrates the importance of child care staff for children.

WHITTAKER, J.K. and TRIESCHMAN, A.E. (1972) *Children Away from Home*, Aldine Atherton.

This book is intended as a source book of residential treatment. The first section comprises a dialogue between the editors on the current issues and problems in residential treatment for emotionally disturbed children. The role and theory of residential treatment are discussed as well as problems relating to staff, communications within the institution, therapy, rules and regulations, punishment, etc.

In the second section of the book the editors have drawn together a collection of readings dealing with the therapeutic milieu for emotionally disturbed children in residential treatment centres. These papers, many of which report research studies, are grouped under the following headings: 1) What is milieu therapy? 2) Individual treatment in a therapeutic milieu 3) Group treatment in a therapeutic milieu 4) The nature of cottage life — strategies for therapeutic interventions 5) Staffing and personnel in a therapeutic milieu 6) The place of activities in a therapeutic milieu 7) Working with the families.

WILLIAMS, C.J. (1972) Helping parents to help their children in placement', *Child Welfare*, 51, 5.

This article describes a residential programme in the United States, designed to meet the needs of a small number of emotionally disturbed school-age children, and considers ways in which parents can be helped to cooperate with the treatment planning.

WOTHERSPOON, C.M.C. (1972) 'Making authority a positive in residential treatment', *Child Welfare*, 51, 10.

This article describes some of the author's experiences in a residential treatment centre for adolescent girls and discusses methods of asserting authority and setting limits in behaviour.

ZIEGLER, S. (1972) 'Residential treatment of emotionally disturbed children in Norway', *Child Welfare*, 51, 5.

A comparison of the residential treatment of emotionally disturbed children in Norway and in the United States.

Milieu therapy is central to residential treatment in Norway where the trend has been away from the American emphasis on individual psychotherapy.

ii) Residential Staff

BANNER, G. (1970a) 'Training for residential social work,' *Community Schools Gazette*, 64, 3.

Following the passing of the Local Authority Social Services Act, this article outlines some of the new proposals for the oversight of training in the entire social work field but with particular reference to residential social work.

BANNER, G. (1970b) 'Leading and caring' (Review of *Leadership in Residential Child Care* by H. Davies Jones), *British Hosptial Journal*, 22nd September.

BARNES, G. (1971) 'Communicating with children: The Child Care Officer's role with children in care', *Child in Care*, 11, 11.

This article discusses the role of the child care officer with children in care and covers some problems of communicating with children of different ages.

BARTER, J. (1970) 'Structural conflict in child care', *British Hospital Journal*, 6th February.

This article considers the frequent conflict which occurs between child care officers and residential workers in children's homes and examines some of the historical and organizational reasons for it. The author suggests that only by developing common values, participating in shared training programmes and raising the status, salaries and conditions of residential workers will a more satisfactory relationship between the two groups of workers be achieved.

DAVIES JONES, H. (1970) *Leadership in Residential Child Care*, National Children's Home.

A convocation lecture of the National Children's Home. This essay provides a general review of residential leadership and while the author draws heavily on his experience of work in an approved school, it is intended to be of general interest to those in the wider fields of residential child care.

The prologue describes, in diary form, a 'fairly normal' day in the life of an Approved School headmaster.

The central theme of the lecture is that current developments in the field of residential child care make preparation for management and leadership roles an indispensable requirement. The author covers the many aspects of leadership, explores their evolution and examines some of the changes which are now required.

Some extracts from a management case study are included in an appendix.

DAVIS, L.F. (1970) 'Time for leisure: its importance to professional standards', *Child in Care*, 10, 9.

This article looks at the relatively poor position of the residential child care officer, compared with the working population, in respect of the time and opportunities available for leisure time.

DIGGLES, M.W. (1970) 'The child care counsellor: new therapist in children's institutions', *Child Welfare*, 49, 9.

An examination of the role of the child care counsellor in the treatment of children in institutions, where the emphasis is shifting from one-to-one therapy to the group living unit as a means of socialization.

HODDER, J. (1970) 'Part-time training', *Child in Care*, 10, 8.

An account of proposals for the course for the award of the Certificate in the Residential Care of Children and Young Persons (part-time course) held at the Southwark College for Further Education, London.

HOLTBY, M.E. (1972) 'Expectations of experienced child care staff', *Child in Care*, 12, 9.

The author suggests that there is a lack of clear-out expectations regarding the skills which child care staff should possess. He provides an itemization of expectations for staff who have one or more year's experience.

The list is specifically concerned with relationships with children and is set out in four sections dealing with — Control; Counselling; General Interaction; Staff Qualities.

HULLEY, T. (1970) 'Coping in Residential Care', *British Hospital Journal*, 80, 4207.

Following the accidental death of a child at Lingfield Hospital School, the author examines some of the problems which are commonplace in residential care including the conditions of service, staff morale and staff turnover.

JILLINGS, J.P. (1967) 'The development of residential work in child care and other fields of residential care', *Care Conference*, 14, 5.

This article suggests that residential work in the child care field and in other branches of social work has not kept pace with developments in the field of professional casework.

Residential child care staff are for the most part untrained. The nature and demands of residential work narrow the field of recruitment, but recruitment is also restricted in quantity and quality by inadequate salary scales.

There can no longer be clear distinctions between social work undertaken in the community and that provided in residential care and as such there seems to be no justification for differences in status and salary between residential and field staff.

Casework and residential staff should share as many aspects of training as possible with linked courses and appropriate lectures shared jointly.

KYDD, R. (1973) 'Training for residential work', *Residential Social Work,* 13, 6.

This article considers some of the changes in the training of residential social workers recommended by the Working Party of the Central Council for Education and Training in Social Work *(qv)*, and discusses their implications.

MAIR, G. (1970) 'Some problems of residential child care', *Child in Care,* 10, 9.

An examination of some of the difficulties in recruiting the right people for residential work. Long hours of work tend to cause staff tension but other contributing factors are frequently poor and cramped staff accommodation and the loneliness and isolation that can be experienced by both houseparents and their assistants.

RACKHAM, K. (1973) 'Communication and support in residential care', *Residential Social Work,* 13, 7.

The needs of residential staff and some of the hazards arising from the nature of their work are considered. The relationship between residential staff and fieldworkers is discussed as well as the problem of inter-staff relationships within the residential setting.

RESIDENTIAL CHILD CARE ASSOCIATION (1968b) *Residential Staff in Child Care,* Annual Review of Residential Child Care Association.

This is a collection of papers written by practitioners and those involved in the training of students for residential work. It examines the role of the residential worker, his and her special responsibilities and the ways in which these can be realistically assessed and deployed.

The review is divided into three parts. The first, which forms half the book, is concerned with the organizational aspects of management and is entitled 'Management — Principles and Practice'. The nine papers in this section deal with the problems imposed on and by the residential setting and cover such topics as recruitment, retirement, training and development, the worker in isolation and the worker in the setting.

The second part — 'Inside the Residential Setting' is concerned with the way in which residential workers learn ways and means of living within the constantly changing residential environment. The third part of the book consists of three papers on 'Residential Student Supervision'.

SCHAFFER, E.B. (1969) 'Isolated in a home', *New Society,* 13, 344.

This article considers the shortage of residential staff and looks at some of the reasons why it has arisen. Among them are poor salary and conditions, and the demands made by the work, but the author holds that the most important reason is the lack of involvement the residential worker has in the care and treatment plan of the child and the lack of support he receives.

TUTT, N. (1974) 'Nature of authority in a residential setting', *Residential Social Work,* 14, 6 & 7.

In these two papers the author analyses the various types of 'power' at work, influencing the behaviour of human beings in their relationships with each other. Five types of power are defined — reward power, coercive power, legitimate power, referent power and expert power — and the operation of these in a residential establishment is then considered.

Residential establishments have traditionally been autocratic institutions with a clearly defined hierarchy of power but this article predicts that the next few years will see 'a marked shift' in the power structure which will lead to individual residential staff having greater authority than previously experienced. It is felt that this will enable them to cope more effectively with the problems presented by the children.

WALTON, R.G. (1968) 'Residential care in children's departments: management by senior staff', *Child Care,* 22, 4.

Following the White Paper *Children in Trouble* which set out machinery for planning residential care services on a regional basis, this article considers the implications of such a planning policy for senior staff. It includes an analysis of the development of residential care in relation to other child care provisions, a description of the methods of organizing residential care with children's departments, an analysis of the technical requirements and an outline of the activities of senior staff.

WINNICOTT, C. (1971) 'The training and recruitment of staff for residential work', *Child in Care,* 11, 1.

The merging of Approved Schools and Children's Homes into a unified system of Community Homes highlights the relationship between education and care. This article discusses the question of training and recruitment for residential work.

In view of the very large numbers of workers urgently needed in the residential field it seems realistic to accept that not all of them could be expected to take a full professional training. Different levels of training must be provided with a clearly defined way for any individual to graduate from one level to the next. The author suggests that a complete professional training programme should consist of four parts:

1. Pre-qualifying in-service study and training,
2. Qualifying training at a college or university,
3. Post-qualifying training by means of internal and external staff development programmes,
4. Advanced courses of study at a university leading to a higher qualification or degree.

iii) The History of Residential Child Care

BANNER, G. (1969) 'Residential care comes of age', *British Hospital Journal*, October 17th.

A discussion of some of the most significant changes that have taken place in residential child care since the Children Act 1948.

BOLMAN, W.M. (1969) 'The future of residential care for children', *Child Welfare*, 48, 5.

This article examines the history of institutional care in America for guidelines in predicting the future of residential care for children.

BOSS, P. (1971) *Exploration into Child Care*, Routledge and Kegan Paul.

This is a study of the main events that have taken place in the development of the child care service in England and Wales during the period between the Curtis Report 1948 and the Seebohm Report 1968.

In its early years it was a comparatively minor social service designed to meet the needs of a defined group of children; its function was mainly a curative one concerned with the child in care or about to come into care. This account details the way in which, over the period, the child care service has gradually shifted its orientation in the direction of the kind of family service foreshadowed in the Seebohm Report of 1968. The final chapter makes some comparisons between child care in 1948 and child care in 1970.

MIDDLETON, N. (1971) *When Family Failed; the Treatment of Children in the Care of the Community in the First Half of the Twentieth Century,* Gollancz.

This sociological study of the treatment of children in care in the first half of this century, was designed to investigate how far those children dependent on the community have fared in comparison with others.

The main material of the book is contained in two accounts of child care at different periods. The first deals with the situation regarding children at the beginning of the century and the operation of the Poor Law; it is based mainly on official reports of the period. The second account deals with the latter part of the period and leans heavily on the Curtis Report of 1946.

The early chapters explore the situation of poor families around 1900, and their dependence upon either the Poor Law or the organized charity system. The welfare apparatus of the period is described to show how the principles and practice of the Poor Law tended to destroy rather than aid families in difficulties and how Victorian attitudes to poverty ignored the pressures on the poor family and the narrow precarious margins on which they lived.

The workhouse situation, its destruction of the family group and the conditions of children are described in detail.

The second phase of the study is concerned with the period from 1918 to the Curtis Report in 1946, and traces the emerging social services during the inter-war years.

The study concludes that, for the unwanted child, change came all too slowly and that in fact, very little change occurred in the half century covered. The popularly accepted progress in the treatment of children had almost completely bypassed those maintained in institutions.

STROSS, G.E. (1970) 'Residential nurseries and the care of young children', *Child Care,* 24, 4.

This article discusses some alternative forms of care for young children (adoption and foster care) and goes on to examine the early history of residential nurseries and development in nursery care which have since taken place.

WALTON, R.G. (1970a) 'Important themes in the development of residential care for deprived children', *Child Care*, 24, 1.

This article examines the changing purpose of residential care for deprived children during this century.

Evidence is cited of the inter-relatedness of demographic, social, technical and policy factors in determining the quality and quantity of residential care available at any one time. Too often in the past policy has developed unrelated to the other factors and although this century has seen the development of an increasingly humane system of children's homes for children in care, steps now need to be taken to make it more effective so that any one child is more likely to receive the type of care suited to his needs.

WALTON, R.G. (1970b) 'Reception Centres', *Child Care,* 24, 2.

An examination of the origins and development of reception centres, from the late nineteenth century to the present day. The growing complexity of their role, including diagnosis and treatment is outlined and the author questions whether these residential observation centres are really necessary, particularly in view of the present scarcity of psychological and psychiatric staff and the fragmentation of diagnosis facilities in the community.

WALTON, R.G. (1969a) 'Residential nurseries', *Child Care*, 23, 4.

This article examines the development of residential nursery care and the changing attitudes towards it, from the beginning of this century to the present day.

WALTON, R.G. (1969b) 'The development of the residential care of deprived children 1900-1965', *Child Care*, 23, 3.

An account of the development of residential child care provision from the beginning of the century. It looks at the numbers of children in care, at the changing proportions in various forms of care and at the policies and pressures that affected these changes. The pattern of development in voluntary care and the numbers of children in different forms of voluntary care are also examined. The most striking changes during this period have been the number of children with both parents alive when admitted to care and the improved state of health of children coming into care.

Following the Second World War the main developments were the gradual reduction of numbers and proportion of children cared for in children's homes after the early 1950s and the reduction in their size, whilst the number of children in family group homes continued to increase.

WHITTAKER, J.K. (1972) 'Group care for children: guidelines for planning', *Social Work*, 17, 1.

An historical analysis of the development of group care in the United States and the implications derived from this for future research and planning. Five topical areas are discussed:

1. Philosophies of child care,
2. Child care institutions as part of the total child welfare,
3. Organization and technology for care and treatment,
4. Group methods of child rearing,
5. The child care institution and the national organization.